Green Gardening

Practical Advice from
National Trust Gardeners

Sue Spielberg

 THE NATIONAL TRUST

First published in Great Britain in 2001
Reprinted in 2002
The National Trust Enterprises Ltd
36 Queen Anne's Gate
London SW1H 9AS
www.nationaltrust.org.uk/bookshop

ISBN 07078 0341 1

Cataloguing in Publication Data is available
from the British Library

Line Drawings by Jim Robins

Designed and typeset in Minion and Frutiger
by the Newton Engert Partnership

Production by Chris Pearson

Printed in Hong Kong by Wing King Tong Ltd

Contents

Introduction

Ten years ago, admitting to gardening organically would have been like confessing at a butchers' convention that you are partial to a nut roast. It would have been viewed with a certain amount of surprise, not to say a suggestion of crankiness. But today, given what we now know about environmental issues such as intensive farming methods, pesticide residues in our food and the threat posed by genetically modified crops, it is no wonder that interest in organic gardening and farming is blossoming. With a membership of 25,000 and rising, the Henry Doubleday Research Association (HDRA), Britain's largest organisation for organic gardening, bears witness to this.

The HDRA's central beliefs are simple, straightforward and downright sensible; to garden without the use of chemicals relies on working with, rather than fighting, nature. This is achieved by feeding the soil rather than the plants, recycling waste, encouraging natural predators to control pests as well as practising good husbandry, which means adhering to crop rotations, clearing away dead and dying foliage and giving plants optimum growing conditions. Most would concede that to garden following organic principles is the model we should all strive for, but in practice it is sometimes too difficult to achieve, and compromises have to be made.

As a high-profile conservation body, the National Trust is a leading light in protecting the environment. It has already resolved to end the use of peat in all its gardens, and it actively promotes composting and recycling of organic materials within its properties. The organic ideal, as laid down by HDRA, is the Trust's preferred goal but given the number and size of the gardens in its guardianship and the slender staff that care for them, pragmatic solutions are called for. For this reason, in all but one of its gardens, the Trust follows the idea of 'integrated pest management', which combines limited chemical use with biological control agents, good cultural methods and physical barriers to limit the spread of pests and diseases. The exception to this is Snowshill Manor in Gloucestershire, which, to date, is the Trust's only true organic garden.

Green Gardening focuses on ten National Trust Head Gardeners (although I could have chosen from countless others) who have their own methods of gardening the environmentally-friendly way. Quite correctly, soil management and composting are emphasised as the secret of all successful gardening – organic or otherwise – lies in the soil. Ways of creating and maintaining varied habitats as well as plants to attract beneficial wildlife are also given. When pests do gain a hold, a wide range of biological controls for indoor and outdoor use is suggested. You will also find ways to control weeds and conserve water as well as tips on companion planting and peat alternatives in potting composts.

With the exception of Linda Roberts at Snowshill Manor, all the gardeners resort to chemicals such as glyphosate, in the absence of alternatives, and use it as a labour-saving way of controlling perennial weeds, particularly on paths. It is still considered to be one of the safest herbicides (if that's not a contradiction in terms), and to minimise further its impact on the environment, glyphosate is always applied using a controlled droplet unit (CDU) to reduce spray drift. Other than that, few other herbicides, and fewer still insecticides, are used because all the gardeners recognise the importance of maintaining the balance of nature; remove just one element and that delicate balance is destroyed.

Given the choice, most of them would prefer not to use any chemicals at all. Let's face it, who in their right mind looks forward to donning the spray suit, goggles and rubber boots that government regulations quite rightly demand? Yet high standards of horticulture expected by the visiting public must be maintained. Rightly or wrongly, National Trust gardens are held up as showcases: to see borders strangled with bindweed or hosta leaves shot through with holes made by slugs and snails is simply unacceptable. The dichotomy for most Head Gardeners – particularly those responsible for large properties – is how to reduce chemical usage without compromising standards. The gardens are invariably run with a small core of staff, so the lack of manpower only serves to exacerbate the situation. As Rob James, former Head Gardener at Glendurgan in Cornwall, so succinctly puts it: 'You try your best to be organic, but within the bounds of standards and financial pressures.'

With my head swimming with tips and ideas from this highly knowledgeable band of gardeners, I set out to put their advice into practice in our own small garden and large allotment. With three lively young boys to bring up, one of my main motives was to supply them with organic vegetables, but as a keen nature lover, I also wanted to encourage as much wildlife to our garden as possible. Time, or rather the lack of it, meant that before my experiment had begun, I had already sprayed both garden and allotment to eradicate perennial weeds. But just a year later I am staggered at how successful the green approach has been.

Although my partner and I spent several Saturday mornings collecting, spreading and digging in mushroom compost to lighten our heavy clay soil, the improvement was rapid and well worth the back-breaking effort. Where it had once been compacted and lifeless, within a few weeks every exploratory spadeful revealed a handful of fat juicy worms. It's no wonder that blackbirds and a thrush soon adopted our garden. Spurred on, I installed a birdbath and strung up an array of birdfeeders with nuts and seeds and watched with delight as bluetits, great tits, gold finches and many others crowded round for a piece of the action.

When we took over the garden two years ago, nothing besides a spectacular Judas tree, an old apple tree and wayward wisteria were worth keeping, so we had the pleasure of starting afresh. My choice of plants always gravitated towards those which would encourage wildlife. Californian poppies, calendulas, bronze fennel, *Verbena bonariensis* and oregano were alive with bees and butterflies, and hoverflies seemed intoxicated by the coriander with its white, cow parsley-like flowers.

But it wasn't all plain sailing. Slugs drove me mad and thwarted every attempt I made to establish hemerocallis, pulmonarias and dahlias. Curiously they never got a taste for the hostas. I discovered that a light dusting of salt on their slimy bodies stopped them in their tracks as well as vented my anger. (Son number three delighted in helping me, earning himself the title of Greatest Slug Hunter in the West!) The situation improved greatly when the soil warmed up enough to apply the slug nematode, which on our heavy soil wasn't until mid-June (see p.78).

To become an organic gardener, you have to undergo a kind of catharsis to arrive at a different level of tolerance. If you don't feel confident enough to dive headlong into the organic ideal, then I would strongly urge you to try your hand at 'green' gardening first. Whether I am strong enough to shun the use of glyphosate on the allotment remains to be seen (how much longer can the dreaded bindweed survive beneath the thick layer of carpet that I hauled over to stifle it?). But I have proved to myself that I do not need to resort to insecticides at the first sniff of trouble. It is generally held that it takes about three years before a natural balance establishes itself in an organic garden, but my experiences of green gardening have shown that benefits are apparent after just one, so there's no point in delaying; the sooner you start, the better.

Chapter 1

Total Organic Gardening

Snowshill Manor, Gloucestershire

At the heart of organic gardening is the desire to avoid the use of chemicals to treat pernicious weeds and everyday garden pests such as slugs, snails and caterpillars. Inevitably, a self-imposed ban on chemical use immediately means that managing your patch becomes more labour intensive – the prospect of hand-weeding and picking off every individual aphid may seem daunting to all but the most committed gardener. However, every insect has a natural predator, and as Linda Roberts of Snowshill Manor in Gloucestershire explains, by creating the right habitats for these predators – be they hedgehogs or birds – you can restore the natural equilibrium of your garden, and harness wildlife to work with you to garden in a greener way.

History of the garden

Area: 0·8 hectares (2 acres)
Soil: neutral-lime/light loam
Altitude: 228m (750ft)
Average rainfall: 660mm (26in)
Average winter climate: very cold

Snowshill Manor is a real gem. Not only does the honey-coloured Cotswold stone house contain one of the most extraordinary collections of collections you are ever likely to see, including a display of Japanese Samurai armour, its garden is equally enchanting. There is a magical timelessness about the place, and on a warm summer evening with the scent of roses heavy in the air, you can almost see the tousle-haired, bespectacled ghost of Charles Paget Wade, its creator, leaning back, pipe in hand, enjoying the fruit of his labours.

Wade, a rather eccentric antiquarian and former architect, purchased Snowshill in 1919 after his return from the Great War, finding the virtually derelict property, complete with its cattleyard and banks of nettles, the perfect antidote to the modern world. Three years later, having restored the manor house for his growing collection of antiques together with a two-roomed outbuilding, the Priest's House, in which he actually lived, he turned his attention to the 0·8 hectare (2 acre) garden. The essence of its design was based on a concept drawn up by the Arts and Crafts architect M. H. Baillie Scott, but Wade chose to simplify some of the fussy details to its considerable benefit.

Dry-stone terraces were built to anchor the garden to the steeply sloping hillside below, and the separate spaces were linked by flights of stone steps and a matrix of paved and gravel paths. The planting is still very informal, consisting of many typical cottage flowers. Tulips, oriental poppies, lupins, foxgloves, alchemilla and roses take centre stage in the early part of the season, before bowing out to phlox, lavender and Japanese anemones. The garden also works on a subconscious level, best illustrated by Wade's skilful manipulation of contrasts: light and dark, sun and shade, hard and soft, formal and informal, simplicity and detail. At every turn there is a new delight. Fortunately for us all Charles Paget Wade donated Snowshill to the National Trust in 1951, five years before his death in 1956.

Linda's background

Linda Roberts has been in charge at Snowshill since 1990. 'Before I was taken on by the Trust, I spent many years working locally as a self-employed gardener. I was initially brought in to do the winter clearance when the previous gardener left, but when the job came up I applied to work here full-time because I liked it so much. It's very friendly and cosy. I like to think that if Charles Paget Wade ever came back, he would be happy with what we have done here,' she says. 'Essentially Snowshill is a relaxed and informal country garden, whose planting is natural and uncontrived. For example, if self-sown evening primroses and foxgloves pop up at the front of the border, that's fine by me, I leave them because it is that type of garden – "ordered chaos" – that's what I call it.'

Organic gardening at Snowshill

At present the garden at Snowhill Manor is the only one looked after by the National Trust that is managed following completely organic principles. The experiment was originally the brainchild of Linda's predecessor, Anna Coombes, who was given the go-ahead on condition that she was able to cope with the increased workload and that standards of maintenance did not decline. Its continuation twelve years on only proves what an outstanding success it has been.

Linda's own philosophy and relaxed attitude obviously helps. 'Everything deserves to live,' she feels, which is why she balks at the thought of applying the parasitic nematode to control slugs. 'The thought of them being eaten from the inside makes me shudder. They are part of the natural cycle and once you interrupt that, you start to break down all we have tried to achieve over the years,' she explains.

Until recently the garden has not been actively promoted as organic. 'When visitors find out, most are usually pleased and find it very interesting,' she says, but she also realises that a small number will try and pick fault in it. Better information to increase visitor awareness will help to explain what is going on and how organic practices affect a garden. For example, one year the large colourful larvae of the mullein moth ravaged a particularly prominent verbascum. 'When I explained that this caterpillar only ate the leaves of verbascum and would not damage anything else, most visitors were pleased I was allowing nature to take its course; others couldn't understand why I didn't get rid of both,' she says. 'I was not just being organic, I was being environmentally friendly at the same time.'

Maintaining the balance of nature

At Snowshill Linda has to walk a tricky tightrope between maintaining a garden that is open to the public and caring for the environment. For example, she would love to delay cutting back the borders until spring to leave hibernating sites for beneficial insects. However, to fit in with her work schedule this has to be accomplished before Christmas thereby leaving adequate time for important development work, which must be completed before the visiting season recommences. 'The important thing is to strike a balance,' she says.

This idea of equilibrium is one of the tenets at the heart of organic gardening – to have a healthy garden you have to encourage as many different forms of life as possible, which means tolerating so-called pests because they are a food source of the gardener's greatest allies. Those generating the best press include birds, hedgehogs, frogs, toads, newts, slow-worms, ladybirds and hoverflies. Less well-known though equally significant predators are ground beetles, centipedes, spiders and wasps. At times the dividing line between friend and foe can be blurred. For example, blackbirds may make short work of ripening cherries but they also guzzle caterpillars and slugs aplenty; similarly wasps may make picnicking hazardous, but early in the season they hunt insects in great numbers.

Refraining from using chemicals is an obvious way to encourage these beneficial creatures, but creating varied habitats and growing appropriate plants will also increase the number and variety of forms of life on your patch. At Snowshill four important habitats are present – ponds, dry-stone walls, hedges and woodland edges – all of them go a long way in helping to enrich the wildlife, and consequently the predator, content in the garden. 'I think the most noticeable change has been the number of birds that are now coming. This is probably because they have realised there is a good supply of food here, and there are lots of places to nest as it is not a manicured garden. Wrens are especially abundant. I keep a list of those I have seen here and already it numbers thirty different species.' Linda continues to reel off a string of birds, the more unusual ones include kestrel, cuckoo, flycatcher, fieldfare, nuthatch, tree creeper, bullfinch, long-tailed tit, buzzard and woodcock.

Pond habitat

Nothing attracts wildlife quite like water; it is by far and away the most important habitat that a gardener can create. Not only does it encourage birds to drink and bathe, toads, frogs and newts require it to breed. The larger the expanse of water the better in terms of its environmental impact, but even the smallest garden can accommodate a bird bath.

Whether you choose to make your own pond using a sheet liner or sink a pre-formed one into the ground, you should bear the following points in mind:

Cross section of an informal pond with several shelves built in at different levels to accommodate a wide range of aquatic and marginal plants.

- Ensure that at some point there is a depth of at least 60cm (2ft) to ensure an ice-free zone for pond life.

- The pond should have at least one gently sloping edge to allow easy access (and exit points) for small and larger creatures. Many a hedgehog has met a grizzly end because it has been unable to get out of the water. You can create a 'beach' in an existing pond by building up a layer of rocks at one edge.

- Fill the pool and allow it to stand for a week or so before stocking it. Add a bucket of water and mud from an established pond for an instant eco-system.

- When furnishing the pond with plants remember to include some oxygenators, such as spiked water-milfoil (*Myriophyllum spicatum*) not to be confused with the invasive *M. aquaticum*, as they supply oxygen and use up excess nutrients in the water that cause blanket-weed and other algae growth. They also provide hiding places for pond creatures. Floating plants, such as frogbit (*Hydrocharis morsus-ranae*) should not be forgotten as they drift on the surface and reduce the amount of sunlight reaching the water. This also curbs the growth of unwanted algae.

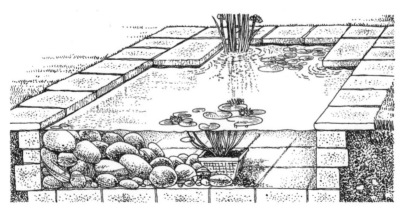

Cross section of a formal pond. Rocks are piled up at one end to create a beach where wildlife can enter and exit.

Removing blanketweed from a pond with a rake.

At Snowshill there are two small garden ponds, both of which are spring-fed. The first formed the harbour of a model fishing village that Charles Paget Wade created. A tiny set of steps down to the water's edge are the only remains of what must have been a most charming feature in its heyday. It is now home to sticklebacks as well as goldfish, and come early spring is often quivering with frog spawn. Submerged oxygenating plants ensure the water is teeming with life, while the surface stays free of growth to enhance the pond's reflective qualities. The Well Court is the setting for the second pond, which is formal and adorned with waterlilies. Neither requires much maintenance on Linda's part apart from raking out the green filamentous growth of blanketweed, which tends to proliferate in sunny weather. She also submerges a bag containing barley straw, which contains a natural algicide, in the ponds in early spring to reduce this problem.

Dry-stone wall habitats

Snowshill boasts a fine matrix of dry-stone walls that are an integral feature of the garden. Although a favourite hiding place for slugs and snails, the damp, cool nooks and crannies within the stones accommodate frogs, toads, mice, spiders and other beneficial insects. Larger crevices make ideal nesting sites for wrens (which probably explains their abundance at Snowshill), robins, great tits, spotted flycatchers and even the redstart, a handsome small bird with striking markings. Dry-stone walls also create their own micro-climate, which tends to be warmer than the surrounding garden, enticing slow-worms, butterflies and hawkmoths to bask in the reflected heat.

Hedge habitat

Hedges not only serve as visual punctuation points and boundaries to the garden, they are also important shelters and corridors for wildlife, allowing creatures to move between gardens and into the countryside beyond. At Snowshill Linda has done her share of hedge planting. Two years ago a hawthorn hedge that used to grow around the property was reintroduced, while a mixed native hedge, made up of blackthorn, hawthorn, hazel, guelder rose and dog rose, has been planted to line the walk from the new car park and restaurant to Charles Paget Wade's original garden.

Before planting a hedge decide on the effect you wish to create, as this will make a difference as to what you actually plant. Do you re-quire a neatly clipped uniform hedge, or one that is more informal, in which the plants are left to grow more naturally to provide a show of flowers and berries? Would a mixed hedge more reminiscent of a countryside hedgerow be more appropriate? Whatever you decide, avoid at all costs conifers such as × *Cupressocyparis leylandii* because there is no way you will contain a tree with a 30m (100ft) soul at a height of 2m (6ft). The table gives suggestions for hedging plants suitable for all soils and their recommended planting distances.

Hedging plants for all soil types

NAME	DESCRIPTION	USE	PLANTING DISTANCE
Acer campestre (field maple)	deciduous; autumn colour	hedgerow	45cm (18in)
Berberis × stenophylla	evergreen; yellow flowers	informal	60cm (24in)
Carpinus betulus (hornbeam)	deciduous; autumn colour	formal	45cm (18in)
Chamaecyparis lawsoniana (Lawson's cypress)	evergreen	formal	60-90cm (24-36in)
Cornus sanguinea (dogwood)	deciduous; white flowers; autumn colour; berries	hedgerow	45cm (18in)
Corylus avellana (hazel)	deciduous; catkins; nuts	hedgerow	45cm (18in)
Cotoneaster simonsii	semi-evergreen; blossom; berries	hedgerow	45cm (18in)
Crataegus monogyna (hawthorn)	deciduous; blossom; berries	hedgerow	45cm (18in)
Euonymus europaeus (spindle)	deciduous; berries	hedgerow	45cm (18in)
Fagus sylvatica (beech)	deciduous; autumn colour	formal	45cm (18in)
Ilex aquifolium (holly)	evergreen; berries	hedgerow & formal	75cm (30in)
Ligustrum ovalifolium (privet)	semi-evergreen	hedgerow & formal	30cm (12in)
Prunus spinosa (blackthorn)	deciduous; blossom; fruit	hedgerow	45cm (18in)
Pyracantha rogersiana (firethorn)	evergreen; blossom; berries	informal	60cm (24in)
Rhamnus cathartica (buckthorn)	deciduous; berries	hedgerow	45cm (18in)
Rosa canina (dog rose)	deciduous; flowers; hips	hedgerow	45cm (18in)
Taxus baccata (yew)	evergreen	formal	45-60cm (18-24in)
Thuja plicata (western red cedar)	evergreen	formal	60-90cm (24-36in)
Viburnum opulus (guelder rose)	deciduous; flowers; berries	hedgerow	45cm (18in)

Woodland edge habitat

In 1993 a new area was created to link the garden with the car park and visitor centre. The walk, which was devised to mimic a sunny woodland edge habitat, provides added interest, but still remains true to the mood of Snowshill.

When the area, known as the Ash Bank, was planted up in 1999, Linda kept in mind the classic woodland structure in which the natural vegetation observes a three-tier system. The topmost layer is made up of larger 'forest' trees; at Snowshill the dominant species is ash. The second layer comprises of smaller trees and woodland shrubs; here randomly planted yew, holly and wild privet provide evergreen structure and winter cover, while hazel, blackthorn, hawthorn and spindle inject added interest in the form of spring flowers and autumn fruit. Climbers, such as honeysuckle and old man's beard (*Clematis vitalba*), go hand in hand with this layer as they scramble onto the backs of neighbouring shrubs in their bid to reach the light. The third layer embraces all those species that thrive on the woodland floor. The majority will be made up of spring flowering opportunists like primroses, dog violets and blue-bells, which surge up to take their chance before the tree canopy closes over for the summer.

In nature each tier will attract an array of animals, birds and insects. Already owls and woodpeckers have taken up residence, along with foxes, weasels, rabbits, toads and frogs. 'We want to attract anything and everything that fancies making a home here,' says Linda with obvious enthusiasm. A fallen tree trunk and several piles of old logs provide yet more habitats, which positively teem with life, helping to further enrich the wildlife content of the area. 'Ultimately we would like to see this as a good thick coppice, which should look natural but not require too much maintenance. We want it to be an added bonus for visitors on their way to the manor.'

Insect boxes

So seriously is Linda taking her new nature reserve that as part of her winter project work she is making up two types of insect boxes which she hopes will attract lacewings, ladybirds, solitary bees or wasps and help them overwinter. One is crammed with bamboo canes and has an open front (a), the other is packed tightly with straw, the insects gaining entry through a wooden front drilled with different-sized holes (b). They are attached to a tree branch or trunk, facing south for winter warmth.

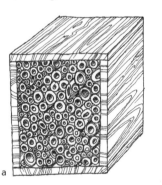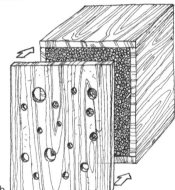

Homemade insect boxes at Snowshill. One is filled with bamboo while the other is tightly packed with straw. Both will help ladybirds, lacewings, solitary bees and other beneficial insects to overwinter in the garden.

Useful wildlife plants at Snowshill

'Anything that provides nectar, berries and cover is excellent for wildlife,' says Linda. Flat, open flowers where the pollen and nectar are fully exposed will attract the greatest range of insects. Plants in the Umbelliferae family, including dill, coriander and fennel, and those belonging to the daisy family, such as asters and sunflowers, are especially attractive to hoverflies, parasitic wasps and other beneficial insects with short mouthparts. The table shows annual and perennial species that have more than proved their worth for wildlife at Snowshill (see also pp.58, 115-16 and 128-9).

Plants for wildlife

PLANT	TYPE/SEASON	WILDLIFE VALUE
Campanula trachelium (nettle-leaved campanula)	perennial/summer to autumn	bees and butterflies
Centranthus ruber (red valerian)	perennial/summer to autumn	hawkmoths, small tortoiseshell
Dipsacus fullonum (teasel)	biennial/mid-summer to autumn	bees and butterflies; seeds for goldfinches
Echinops ritro (globe thistle)	perennial/late summer	bees and butterflies; seeds for finches
Echium vulgare 'Blue Bedder'	biennial/summer	bees
Limnanthes douglasii (poached egg plant)	annual/early to late summer	bees and hoverflies
Nepeta (catmint)	perennial/mid- to late summer	bees
Oenothera biennis (evening primrose)	biennial/mid- to late summer	bees, hoverflies and moths; seeds for finches
Phlox paniculata	perennial/summer	butterflies and moths
Reseda odorata (mignonette)	annual/summer to early autumn	bees, butterflies and caterpillars
Salvia viridis (syn. *S. horminum*) (annual clary)	annual/summer	bees
Sedum spectabile (iceplant)	perennial/autumn	bees and butterflies
Solidago canadensis (golden rod)	perennial/autumn	butterflies; seeds for finches
Verbena bonariensis	perennial/summer to late autumn	butterflies

Fruits and berries

One of the best ways of attracting a wide range of birds to the garden is to provide them with berrying plants. Many of the trees and shrubs at Snowshill and in the surrounding countryside produce bountiful crops of fruits and berries, arousing a flurry of activity throughout the autumn and winter months. Some of the most notable are outlined below:

Berberis thunbergii **f.** *atropurpurea* A small deciduous shrub, growing to about 1·2m (4ft) tall, with purplish-bronze foliage that turns red in autumn. The tiny glossy fruits sparkle like red jewels on the naked twiggy branches and last well into the winter.

Cotoneaster lacteus A dense evergreen shrub or small tree with arching branches, about 4m (12ft) tall. Its red berries last well into the winter.

Crataegus monogyna (**hawthorn**) An invaluable small deciduous tree, growing to 8m (25ft). Clouds of white blossom appear in early summer, followed by red berries, greedily pilfered as soon as they are ripe in late autumn.

Hedera helix (**common ivy**) A hardy evergreen climber, growing up to 30m(100ft), with yellow-green insignificant flowers that supply nectar to hoverflies and butterflies, especially the holly blue and tortoiseshells. Green berries turn black when ripe and are voraciously eaten by resident birds and winter visitors. Its thick mantle also provides nesting sites for wrens, sparrows and blackbirds.

Lonicera periclymenum (**honeysuckle or woodbine**) A deciduous climber, growing up to 6m (20ft). Beautiful, highly scented, purple-tinged flowers, beloved by hawkmoths and bumble bees, appear in summer. In autumn the red berries are eaten by a variety of birds.

Wild and species shrub roses Deciduous prickly shrubs, growing 2m (6ft) and more. Mostly cultivated for their glorious summer blooms, many are blessed with autumn hips as well, which are especially attractive to birds, foxes and wood mice. Good species for wildlife are: *R. rugosa* with large orange-red hips; *R. glauca* with slim dark red hips; and *R. rubiginosa*, or sweet briar, with apple-scented foliage when crushed and bright red hips.

***Symphoricarpos albus* var. *laevigatus* (snowberry)** A thicket-forming deciduous shrub, growing to 2m (6ft). Succulent, round, long-lasting, pure white fruits, beloved by blackbirds follow its tiny pink flowers.

***Viburnum opulus* (guelder rose)** A deciduous shrub, growing to 4m (12ft) high, with fine autumn colour. Its creamy white flowers in early summer are followed by pendant clusters of shining scarlet berries.

Pests and diseases

At Snowshill there is little direct intervention on Linda's part to control pests and diseases, she prefers instead to let nature take its course. 'You have got to be patient to let the beneficial wildlife build up in the first place, and it will do the job for you.' She also thinks a change in attitude must be made before a conventional gardener is ready to shun the use of chemicals. 'You will never make a successful organic gardener if you always rush to get the spray at the first glimpse of greenfly.'

But here's the rub: some plants, no matter how hard you try to prevent it, attract pests and diseases like a magnet. At Snowshill Linda cites blackspot on *Rosa* 'Albertine' and slugs and snails on the hostas in the Well Court as her examples. 'You've either got to learn to live with them or if you can't then you've no alternative but to dig up the plants and replace them with something more pest- or disease-resistant,' she declares.

Coping with weeds

The backbone of gravel paths and paving stones at Snowshill is sheer heaven for garden visitors, eager to explore and discover what lies in the 'rooms' beyond, but they can be a real headache when it comes to keeping them weed-free. As an organic practitioner, Linda cannot rely on the usual weedkillers most non-organic gardeners would resort to, so until now there has been no other alternative but to weed them by hand – a lengthy and time-consuming option. However, another avenue may be opening soon. 'We're looking at buying a flame weeder. It will be expensive initially, but I think it could be well worth it. Most people expect to get a good kill the first time they use a flame weeder, but the most effective way is not to try and burn them all off in one session. Instead they should swish over the weeds, leave them for about a week and then repeat the procedure. Doing it twice should kill all the weeds and put pay to their seeds,' Linda advises.

The only other weed problem at Snowshill concerns a small patch of ground elder and bindweed in one of the borders. Pragmatic as ever, Linda digs them out as best she can when the first fingers prick through the soil. 'It is impossible to get out all the roots because they are growing right behind a rose; I simply try to contain them.'

Making compost

As all organic gardeners are aware, the secret of success lies in the soil. Keep it in good heart by applying plenty of organic matter, and it will reward you, but disregard it at your peril. Organic matter, in the form of well-rotted farmyard manure, home-made garden compost or leafmould (to name but a few), is the elixir of life and will feed the vital soil-living creatures and microbes. These in turn break down the matter into nutrients that the plants can absorb, and healthy plants are better able to withstand pest and disease attack than sickly ones.

For this reason making compost comes high on Linda's list of priorities. 'Anything I can get my hands on will be put back onto the garden in the form of compost,' she laughs. This includes all the grass clippings and shredded prunings from the garden, as well as shredded paper from the property office and vegetable waste from the restaurant, for all the staff support the environmental principles at work at Snowshill. It also includes pigeon guano from the dove-cote, which is added in layers and doubles as a compost activator. Linda feels the end product not only conditions the soil, it also feeds it because it is so rich in nutrients (see also pp.50, 88 and 111).

On average slightly over half the garden receives a blanket of mulch in winter, generated from the five wooden compost bins on site. The rest will be treated to home-made leafmould. Both are applied to a depth of 5cm (2in) after the borders have been 'put to bed' for winter. 'I always liken the process of making compost to a good cake: not too wet, not too dry with a good mix of ingredients. You should try to combine dry materials such as prunings, with moister ones like grass clippings so they react together,' Linda explains. She never has time to turn the heap, as is often recommended, but this does not seem to matter. 'However, when I start using it on the borders, I always make sure I take off the top layer and use this to start a new bin. That way all the worms and micro-organisms are ready to go.'

Roughly chopping prunings prior to composting will speed up the decomposition process.

Tips

- No matter how big your garden you can still do your bit to attract wildlife, even if it is just by adding a berrying shrub. 'Every little bit helps, particularly when seen as part of a whole. Imagine a row of houses – if those householders planted just one plant in their garden to attract wildlife that would soon add up to have a big impact on the surrounding environment,' says Linda.

- If blackspot is a constant scourge on your roses why not try out the following remedy, which is thought to work because animal manure contains phenol compounds disliked by fungi. Put one part well-rotted garden compost (a component of which should have been animal manure) in a sack and immerse it in six parts water. Allow to stand for a week before straining the liquid for use. Apply to the foliage with a sprayer or watering can fitted with a fine rose. This must be repeated every five or six days to be effective.

- Do not overfeed your borders, especially with nitrogen, as this produces too much sappy growth, which is then vulnerable to pest and disease attack.

- Refrain from watering in the summer unless absolutely necessary. Once you start you must carry on because the roots start coming up to the surface, and are then put at even greater risk from drying out. If you do have to irrigate, give plenty of water at one time. Don't do it little and often.

- Save your own rainwater by putting up guttering around your shed or greenhouse and allowing it to fill a water butt or similar large container. At Snowshill Linda has gone one stage further. Gutters around the greenhouse allow rainwater to fill an old cattle trough outside before being fed by the overflow into a water tank already set in place inside. This system ensures a more or less constant supply of rainwater in the greenhouse, which is maintained at the ambient temperature.

- Try to seek out pest- and disease-resistant cultivars whenever you buy plants.

- Allow the odd clump of nettles to grow in an out-of-the-way corner as caterpillar food for butterflies; small tortoiseshells, peacocks, commas, and red admirals all rely on nettle leaves for their survival.

- Roughly cut up prunings from the garden before putting them into the wheelbarrow. This saves time at the compost heap, and prevents having to handle them twice. However, avoid composting diseased material, perennial weeds such as bindweed, or anything too woody. As a general rule, if it is too large to go through a shredder it should be burnt and not composted.

Chapter 2

The Organic Kitchen Garden

Clumber Park, Nottinghamshire

Vegetables are among the most labour intensive crops to cultivate at the best of times, but what can be more satisfying than consuming home-grown organic fruit and veg? Good soil and a healthy pragmatic attitude are essential ingredients for success. As Neil Porteous of Clumber Park in Nottinghamshire points out, it's not the end of the world if your apples are blemished, but you will need to take action if your crops come under siege from rabbits or are threatened by carrot root fly. Here he suggests how to make the most of your soil by sensible crop rotation and using green manures, while deterring those hungry rabbits by using the plants they most dislike.

History of the garden

Area: 10·5 hectares (26 acres)
Soil: acid/sandy
Altitude: 30m (100ft)
Average rainfall: 609mm (24in)
Average winter climate: cold

Enter Clumber Park under the impressive Apley Head Gate and drive through the magnificent, curving, 2 mile (3·2km) long double avenue of lime trees, and a tingling feeling of great expectation starts to well up inside. Whatever lies beyond must be as grand and as breathtaking as the approach route. The surprise is bittersweet. No great house to speak of, since all but the study was demolished in 1938 after a fire, but the bones of an eighteenth-century pleasure garden, together with its substantial walled kitchen garden, still remain. True, the loss of the house creates a void since it deprives the park of its *raison d'être*, but there is a wealth of other garden features to fill up on.

At its heart is a long serpentine lake, created by damming the River Poulter in the 1760s. On one side a long terrace walk through specimen trees and shrubs leads to the remains of a dock where a pleasure boat was once moored; on the other oaks, limes and other broad-leaved trees frame a temple and create rippling reflections in the water. An ornate Gothic Revival chapel made from warmly-coloured Runcorn stone now serves as a focal point in the garden in the absence of a house. Leading from the informal pleasure garden, a shady path lined with cedars opens out through wrought iron gates onto the extensive walled kitchen garden. The course of the path rises up on a shallowly sloping gradient, lined in part by sublime herbaceous borders, to be punctuated at the end by a splendid glasshouse range, framed by the brick-built estate office behind.

The history of Clumber is one of mixed fortunes, having huge sums of money ploughed into it, followed by periods of cost cutting. For over 160 years it belonged to the Dukes of Newcastle. First to stamp his signature on the property was the 2nd Duke, who was given Clumber by his uncle as a divertissement following the death of his wife. From the 1760s to 1794 the pleasure grounds, walled kitchen gardens and glass range were created. Having married a rich heiress in 1807, the 4th Duke also lavished a fortune on the estate until the 1840s, developing the terrace adjacent to the house. The 6th Duke was declared bankrupt in 1869 and barred from living at Clumber, and it was not until the marriage of the 7th Duke in 1889 that the fate of the gardens took an upturn. The kitchen gardens underwent major renovation, and the central portion of the Long Range, known as the Palm House, was erected. However these halcyon days were destined not to last; after the death of the 7th Duke in 1927, Clumber, along with his Newark, Nottingham and Worksop estates, was purchased by the London and Fort George Land Company. During the Second World War the kitchen garden was used by the Women's Land Army as a market garden, and in 1946 Clumber Park was sold to the National Trust.

Neil's background

Neil Porteous was taken on as Head Gardener in February 1999, on the retirement of his predecessor, Brian Wilde. Listening to his CV, his previous jobs have obviously stood him in good stead for forthcoming projects at Clumber. These included a stint at Hilliers Nursery in Hampshire and at Bristol Zoo. He then took charge of the organically-run Churchill Court in Somerset, before taking a degree in landscape management. His final port of call before coming to Clumber was the walled garden at Normanby Hall near Scunthorpe in Lincolnshire, which uses a blend of traditional and organic methods of cultivation.

Neil has a fondness for old gardening books, such as *The Forcing Garden* by Samuel Wood (1885), and an enviable talent for recalling snippets of information gleaned from them. Did you know that hedgehogs were recommended to keep woodlice at bay in the Mushroom House? Or that they used to dig deep pits in the ground in order to make leafmould? But he is equally interested in modern gardening, which is just as well because one of his projects in the walled kitchen garden is to grow and compare old-fashioned cultivars of vegetables alongside the modern F1 hybrids.

'Although I'm interested in vegetables, my specialities are trees and shrubs. My main passion is to get hold of this garden and put it back to how it might have looked at the beginning of the twentieth century, bearing in mind all the elements from its 240 years of history. For example, it would be nice to put back some of the early exotics from North America and China, introduced to Clumber around 1765, as well as redefining the island beds in the Pleasure Ground to accommodate its many Victorian elaborations. The challenge is to make all that seem like a natural progression without spoiling what we already have.'

Organic gardening at Clumber

Neil and his staff of two are responsible for approximately 10 hectares (24 acres) of the entire Clumber estate, which comprises of around 1,539 hectares (3,800 acres) of wood and parkland, carved out of Sherwood Forest in Nottinghamshire. Given the size of the garden and the limited manpower available, only the kitchen garden is to be run organically. 'Brian [Wilde] started it, I am simply carrying on where he left off. Our approach may not be strictly endorsed by the Soil Association, for example in winter we spray a weak solution of Armillatox onto the vines and figs in the Long Range. But we do not want to use straight chemicals either. We would like to go our own way as far as possible, and be as true to ourselves as we can.'

Outside the walled kitchen garden the only chemical that is tolerated is glyphosate, a systemic herbicide which is said to become harmless on contact with the soil, and even that is applied with a controlled droplet applicator to minimise spray drift. No residual weedkillers are allowed because the whole area has been designated a Site of Special Scientific Interest (SSSI) for perching and songbirds; among others the rare hawfinch is resident on the estate.

The kitchen garden at Clumber

At present only a third of the 2.4-hectare (6-acre) walled kitchen garden, which dates from 1772, is being cultivated. It is hoped that by 2004 the entire enclosure will once again be worked, with produce going to the visitor restaurant. It does not claim to be an historically accurate restoration, rather a practical interpretation to fit in with the present workload. Neil's natural optimism is tempered by realism when explaining his hopes for Clumber. 'Whatever we do has to be sustainable. Vegetables are very labour intensive, that is why we are using easily mown grass paths around the beds to cut down on labour.'

Importance of crop rotation

All good vegetable gardeners will expound the benefits of crop rotation whereby closely related vegetables or those requiring similar soil and nutrient requirements are kept together and grown on a different patch of soil each year. In practice this usually means dividing the site into three or four equal sections so that a given crop does not return to the same spot for three or four years. This has three benefits: to maintain soil fertility, to reduce pest and disease build-up and to improve soil structure.

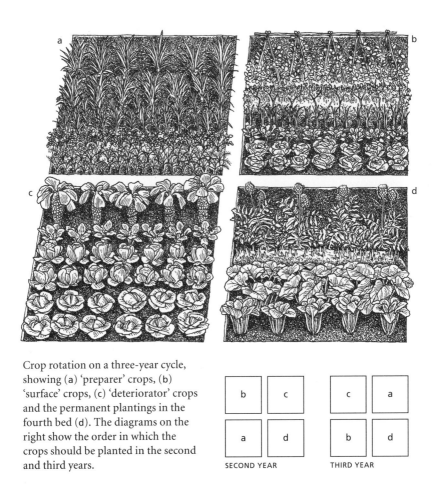

Crop rotation on a three-year cycle, showing (a) 'preparer' crops, (b) 'surface' crops, (c) 'deteriorator' crops and the permanent plantings in the fourth bed (d). The diagrams on the right show the order in which the crops should be planted in the second and third years.

b	c
a	d

SECOND YEAR

c	a
b	d

THIRD YEAR

So far, a total of eight beds, four each side of the central gravel path, have been laid out in the kitchen garden. Neil plans to adopt a three-year crop rotation, with the fourth bed given over to permanent vegetables such as asparagus, seakale, globe artichokes and rhubarb on one side of the path, and soft fruit on the other (d). Traditionally, the succession of crops would have been as follows:

1st year – 'preparer' crops such as carrots, parsnips, potatoes, onions, salsify and scorzonera. A small amount of well-rotted manure would have been laid down in trenches three spits deep, causing roots to grow down in search of moisture (a).

2nd year – 'surface' crops such as lettuce, radish, spring onions and all the legumes (peas and beans). Moderate amounts of well-rotted manure would have been laid down in shallow trenches one spit deep (b).

3rd year – 'deteriorator' crops, which include all the members of the brassica family (eg. cabbages, cauliflower, broccoli and Brussels sprouts, turnips). Generous amounts of well-rotted manure would have been applied in trenches two spits deep (c).

Improving sandy soil with organic matter

Clumber estate lies on inherently infertile heathland but over the centuries the soil structure has been much improved, and can now be described as an acidic to neutral sandy loam, which is gloriously workable most of the time, even after heavy rain. 'The soil hereabouts is very droughty and requires an awful lot of input to enrich it', explains Neil. 'Old gardening books say that you need to apply 100 tons per acre of land to build a sandy soil by about ¼in per annum. That is a lot of manure!' So far, each of the new vegetable beds has soaked up five trailer loads of manure and three of mushroom compost. It is likely to be a similar story in subsequent years.

At first Neil found the manure difficult to incorporate with a rotovator as it was very slimy. However, through trial and error he discovered that spreading it on the surface and lightly turning it in with a spade prior to rotovating allowed the blades of the machine to break it up more effectively. Better still was when spent mushroom compost was placed on top. Carried out in spring, this double whammy not only improves soil structure but also increases its fertility.

Green manures

Another way of improving the soil's fertility and structure is to use a technique known as green manuring, which involves selecting an appropriate crop (or green manure) to suit the soil type and time of year, and broadcasting it over spare ground. When the area is needed again and while the growth is still young and sappy, the entire crop is dug back into the soil. Green manures are particularly effective on poor sandy soils, like those at Clumber, as they lock up the nutrients in the ground, and prevent them from being leached out with the winter rains. The table overleaf lists the most commonly used ones.

Digging in green manure while the growth is still young and leafy.

Green manures

NAME	TYPE	SOWING TIME	COMMENTS
*Alfalfa (*Medicago sativa*) ·	Perennial	Spring – mid-summer	Avoid acid soil. Deep rooting. Foliage rich in nutrients, can be cut and composted or used as a mulch.
Buckwheat (*Fagopyrum esculentum*)	Annual	Spring – late summer	Tolerates poor soils. Dig 2–3 months after sowing. Pink flowers attract hoverflies.
*Essex red clover (*Trifolium pratense*)	Short-lived perennial	Mid-spring – late summer	Unsuitable for acid soil. Good for bees if allowed to flower.
*Fenugreek (*Trigonella foenum-graecum*)	Annual	Early spring – late summer	Rapid grower. Dig 2–3 months after sowing. Best green manure for summer use.
Grazing rye (*Secale cereale*)	Annual	Late summer – late autumn	Best green manure for over-wintering. Its dense roots benefit soil structure.
*Lupin (*Lupinus angustifolius*)	Annual	Early spring – early summer	Good for light acid soils. Sow in rows. Poor weed suppressor.
Mustard (*Sinapis alba*)	Annual	Spring – late summer	Fast-growing. Susceptible to clubroot so should be used with care in crop rotations. Best dug in as a seedling.
Phacelia (*Phacelia tanacetifolia*)	Annual	Early spring – late summer	Easy to incorporate. Flowers loved by bees and hoverflies.
Poached egg plant (*Limnanthes douglasii*)	Hardy annual	Early spring – late summer	Good weed suppressor. Easy to incorporate. Flowers loved by bees and insects.
*Trefoil (*Medicago lupulina*)	Biennial	Early spring – late summer	Good for light but not acid soil. Tolerates some shade.
*Winter tares (*Vicia sativa*)	Hardy annual	Early to late spring or mid- to late summer	Avoid acid and dry soils. Good nitrogen fixer and weed suppressor. Sow in rows.

Those marked with * are known as legumes and are able to fix nitrogen from the air in the nodules on their roots, helping to improve soil fertility.

Liquid feeds

Comfrey Neil intends to plant great swathes of comfrey, or sym-phytum, beneath the north-facing borders. Its tubular flowers, in shades of white, pink, mauve and blue are beloved by bees, and its leaves, if packed into a container and steeped in water make a nutrient-rich liquor; hungry plants such as tomatoes lap it up. It may be a touch smelly, but what it lacks in aroma it more than makes up for in efficacy. Be warned though, once planted you will never be rid of comfrey; its brittle tap roots snap easily, so only dare to plant it in an odd corner of the garden or as a groundcover beneath established trees and shrubs.

Russian comfrey (*Symphytum × uplandicum*), although a thug, offers the best credentials to organic gardeners. Once established, the plants can be cut and cropped four or five times a season. As well as making a liquid feed rich in nitrogen and potassium, its foliage can be cut and added to the compost heap as an activator, or used as a fertility mulch around hungry feeders. A word of advice though: wear gloves when handling the plant as its hairy leaves can irritate the skin.

Making a nutrient-rich liquid feed by suspending a sack of comfrey leaves in a barrel of water.

Animal dung Similarly malodorous is sheep, cow or horse dung, suspended in hessian sacks in a barrel of water for two weeks.

Pelleted chicken manure This is a product that many Trust gardeners have taken to heart. The raw material can be sprinkled over the borders in spring, but Neil also uses it to make an effective liquid feed for pot plants. He simply adds about two handfuls to some warm water, and once dissolved, he further dilutes it until it resembles 'the colour of weak tea'.

Unusual Vegetables

Future special events planned for Clumber include a series of themed dinners to be held in the Palm House of the Long Range. Neil's intention is to supply old-fashioned and unusual vegetable varieties freshly harvested from the kitchen garden. He has tasted them all, with varying degrees of success. Elecampane (*Inula helenium*), for example, was supposed to have been a substitute for carrots in Elizabethan times, its yellow roots turning blue on cooking, but Neil was far from enamoured. 'They are the filthiest things you have ever tasted,' he affirms. 'But I'm still alive that's the main thing. Traditional gardeners knew perfectly well how to grow these strange crops but most would never have eaten them.' Others he hopes to be growing are:

Bulbous-rooted chervil Chervil is usually cut for its leaves, but this form is like a short parsnip.

Chinese artichokes Perennial grown for its knobbly white tubers which have a nutty taste.

Couve tronchuda (Portuguese cabbage) Very loose cabbage, which when boiled, does not smell unpleasant. The long white leaf stalks can be used as a substitute for seakale. Hence two vegetables for the price of one.

Good King Henry (*Chenopodium bonus-henricus*) Perennial with juicy leaves that can be eaten like spinach. Young shoots can be blanched and used like asparagus.

Okra or ladies' fingers (*Hibiscus esculentus*) Annual grown for its ribbed, fleshy, pointed, dark green seed pods, useful in Indian cuisine.

Quinoa (*Chenopodium quinoa*) Annual grown for its nutritious seeds and its tender young foliage.

Rampion (*Campanula rapunculus*) Grown for its white, carrot-shaped, winter roots.

Rocambole (*Allium scorodoprasum*) A form of garlic that resembles a daffodil bulb. It was recommended to ladies because it did not taint the breath. 'I tried it once and my stomach felt as though it was on fire; I was nearly sick. I later learnt that it doesn't produce its mild edible bulbils until its second year!'

Skirret (*Sium sisarum*) Grown for its numerous fleshy roots, rather like slender dahlia tubers.

Tropaeolum tuberosum An attractive climber with the bonus of hot peppery leaves and flowers, as well as a fleshy edible root.

Pests at Clumber

Despite its utilitarian past, few vegetables have been grown at Clumber in the last thirty years. As such, Neil has little idea what pests and diseases, if any, may befall such a fledgling kitchen garden. He maintains a relaxed attitude to possible problems – why worry unless a particular one arises, and is it that serious anyway? Most people can live with the odd blemish on an apple, but when carrot root fly threatens to ruin the whole crop, action will obviously be necessary. Careful observation is a key to success when growing fruit and vegetables organically, that way any infestation can be nipped in the bud and dealt with accordingly. 'They say carrots are one of the most difficult crops to grow well, so if we can grow them, we will be laughing,' says Neil optimistically.

Below is a list of common problems that Neil may encounter in the kitchen garden, as well as his suggestions for controlling them:

Aphids Often referred to as greenfly or blackfly. These cause damage in three ways: they reduce the plant's vigour by sucking its sap; the 'honeydew' they excrete causes sooty mould which cuts down the light reaching the foliage; some aphids transfer viruses from plant to plant. Natural predators such as birds, hoverflies, ladybirds and spiders are the best defence, but if numbers build up insecticidal soap will help (see also p.135).

Cabbage root fly Small, brown housefly-like insect lays its eggs near the brassica stem, the resultant grubs then eat the roots of the plant causing it to wilt and die. Either drape horticultural fleece over the crop after planting or place a collar of carpet underlay, 15cm (6in) in diameter, around each transplant to prevent the adult getting near its base. Traditionally a rhubarb leaf placed in the hole before planting the young brassica was thought to deter the fly since it released an unpleasant smell as it decomposed.

Carrot root fly Shiny black insect, similar to a housefly, that lays its eggs near carrot stems; the resultant grubs then tunnel into the tap roots. A physical barrier such as horticultural fleece laid over the crop is the most effective prevention. Since the adult is attracted by

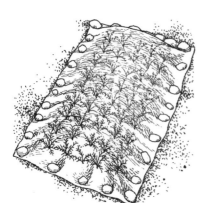

Laying horticultural fleece over a carrot crop can provide an effective physical barrier against the carrot root fly.

smell, sowing thinly to alleviate the need for thinning will also help, as will growing onions nearby (see p.65). Paraffin, according to one of Neil's old references is also effective because its smell confuses the fly. Either soak a length of string in paraffin and tension it 30cm (12in) above the soil, or soak small heaps of sawdust in it and place them 30cm (12in) apart along the row.

Caterpillars Most can be picked off by hand but if infestations do occur spray with the bacterial control, *Bacillus thuringiensis*, which will only kill caterpillars. A wetting agent such as Agral will improve its efficacy on brassicas by breaking the surface tension of the water. Spraying the undersides of the leaves is particularly effective.

Codling moth Grubs of this moth invade developing fruits, leaving messy tunnels inside. Pheromone traps, put in place in mid-May will trap the male moth, resulting in fewer eggs being laid.

Grey mould (*Botrytis cinerea*) Very common disease that affects all plants, causing a fluffy grey mould on fruit, flowers, leaves and stems. If disturbed, clouds of spores are released. It is worse in damp, cool weather. Good growing conditions and hygiene are the best prevention. Avoid overwatering and ensure good ventilation in glasshouses in winter and spring. Spraying with pure sulphur or Bordeaux mixture (made up of copper sulphate and slaked lime) will help prevent the disease spreading to unaffected plants.

Mildew Two main types occur: powdery mildew, which causes a white powdery coating on stems and leaves particularly in hot, dry weather; and downy mildew, which causes brown patches on the upper leaf surface accompanied by grey or purple mould on the underside and is worse in warm, damp weather. Good growing conditions and pruning are the best prevention, but spraying with sulphur or Bordeaux mixture will also help.

Slugs and snails Ubiquitous creatures that leave shredded, nibbled foliage and trails of slime in their wake. Vulnerable plants are seedlings, young vegetables and emerging herbaceous foliage, with damage often worse in mild, damp conditions. Encouraging their natural predators such as birds, frogs, hedgehogs and ground beetles is the best form of defence, but you can also trap them in down-turned orange or grapefruit shells or saucers containing diluted beer. Picking them off is also effective. Once the soil temperature is above 5°C (40°F), usually from mid-April onwards, you can water on a microscopic nematode, available from specialist suppliers, which is a naturally occurring slug parasite (see p.78).

Wireworm Neil suspects that wireworms, the larvae of the click beetle, may be a problem in potato tubers, as they are normally the most significant pest in soil reclaimed from grassland, but their numbers tend to decrease naturally over three or four years with thorough cultivation.

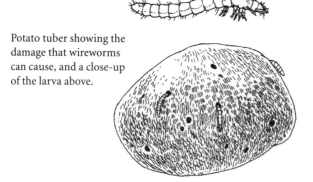

Potato tuber showing the damage that wireworms can cause, and a close-up of the larva above.

Rabbits

Enjoying as it does a rural position, Clumber has its fair share of rabbit trouble. A couple of cats on the property help to keep down the burgeoning numbers, as do a resident population of stoats and weasels. Curious by nature, rabbits will often nibble newly planted specimens. The best defence in a small garden is to fence them out entirely using wire netting, buried at least 15cm (6in) below the ground, with 75cm (30in) above soil level. Where this is impossible, protect individual plants with wire netting until they have become established. Neil has now compiled a list of subjects particularly disliked by rabbits.

Shrubs	Perennials
Aucuba	Aconitum
Berberis	Aster
Box	Astilbe
Choisya	Buphthalmum
Cornus	Epimedium
Cotoneaster	Paeonia
Daphne	Papaver
Eleagnus	Sedum
Rosemary	

Plants that attract wildlife

The long herbaceous borders that line the central path of the kitchen garden at Clumber have been replanted recently with plants that peak mainly from mid-July through to August. On making his selection, Neil was mindful to select those with a value to wildlife. Notable examples are listed below, with key plants such as verbascum and nepeta being repeated at intervals to give the beds a feeling of continuity and rhythm:

Anthemis tinctoria 'E. C. Buxton' Lemon-yellow daisy-like flowers; 45–70cm (18–28in) tall.

Aster amellus 'King George' Large violet-blue daisy-like flowerheads; 45cm (18in) tall.

Aster × *frikartii* 'Mönch' Long-lasting lavender-blue flowers on strong stems; 70cm (28in) tall.

Nepeta **'Six Hills Giant'** Abundant spikes of lavender-blue flowers, beloved by bees and butterflies; to 90cm (36in) tall, good for the front of a border.

Penstemons Foxglove-like tubular flowers in shades of pink, red, white, mauve and blue; anything up to 75cm (30in) tall.

Phlox paniculata **cultivars** Fragrant, white or pale to dark lilac flowers; to 1·2m (4ft) tall.

Rudbeckia **'Herbstsonne'** Large clear yellow, daisy-like flowers; to 2m (6ft) tall, good for the back of a border.

Sedum spectabile Flat heads of tiny star-like pink flowers, beloved by bees and butterflies; 50cm (20in) tall.

Sidalcea **'Rose Queen'** Funnel-shaped mid-pink flowers; 90cm (36in) tall.

Verbascum chaixii **'Gainsborough'** Spikes of soft yellow flowers; to 1·2m (4ft) tall.

Organic management in the Long Range

The *pièce de resistance* in the kitchen garden is the magnificent greenhouse known as the Long Range. Completed in 1908 and measuring 137m (450ft), it is the longest in Trust ownership. Two long wings, each with five bays, radiate from the taller central portion; vines and figs dominate the western section, peaches and nectarines the eastern one. Growing under glass obviously broadens the spectrum of plants that can be cultivated but it also creates an artificial environment in which the balance of nature can be easily upset, with the scales tipped heavily in favour of pests and diseases.

Neil manages the entire glasshouse at Clumber as organically as possible but admits there are problems. 'Last year the figs were hooching with mealybugs.' Due to the unavailability of other

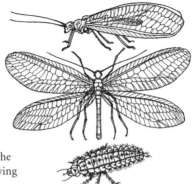

Close-up of
Chrysoperla carnea, the
common green lacewing
and its larva.

predators, he introduced the larvae of the common green lacewing
(*Chrysoperla carnea*), which is a non-specific predator that will
attack sucking insects as well as aphids. 'They are vicious little
things. You have to space them out otherwise they would eat each
other. They'd even take a lump out of your finger!' he jokes. They
were moderately successful but this year Neil is taking no chances.
He has rallied his troops; the more usual mealybug predator,
Cryptolaemus, will spearhead the counter attack, with back-up from
two species of parasitic wasp – *Leptomastix epona* and *L. dactylopii*
– which seek out the vine mealybug and citrus mealybug respectively. See also p.135.

   To be effective minimum temperatures must reach 16°c (61°F), so
the introduction of biological controls begins in early July and goes
on once a month until the end of September. 'It takes nerves of steel
not to resort to chemicals, particularly early in the season before the
control has been put in place,' admits Neil. 'On the whole, though,
public reaction is positive once we explain what we are trying to do.'

Advantages of biological controls

- Many common pests and diseases such as red spider mite and whitefly have now become resistant to whole classes of pesticides, so their

efficacy is at best limited, at worst ineffectual. As long as their prey is present, biological agents will work.

- The majority of biological controls are host-specific, leaving other (and often beneficial) insects unharmed.

- There is no need to don protective gear in order to apply them.

- There will be no chemical residues on food.

- They minimise ecological damage and are safer for the environment.

Disadvantages

- Most require warm conditions to be effective. This varies from 14-25°C (57-77°F), depending on the insect being used, so they are unsuitable for use early in the growing season.

- Biological controls are sensitive to pesticide residues up to ten weeks after spraying. Therefore a method of control, such as insecticidal soap, must be sought in the interim.

- They are expensive. At Clumber Neil spends about £800 each year on the biological controls alone.

- In most cases, pest levels are reduced to an acceptable level, but rarely wiped out completely.

Water conservation at Clumber

To support a range of vegetables, the free-draining sandy loam at Clumber needs to be irrigated periodically during dry spells throughout summer. An ingenious watering system, combining the best of high and low technology, safeguards against drought. The run-off from the roof ensures thousands of gallons of water are collected in the original matrix of water tanks below the Long Range and utilised to feed the modern irrigation system outside. A permeable length of hose, known as leaky pipe, is laid in straight lines below the vegetable beds, while sprinklers hidden in the lawn pop up at the touch of a button to water the herbaceous borders.

Tips

- As it has no residual effects, insecticidal soap is a useful and permissible pesticide against whitefly, aphids and red spider mite for organic gardeners when the going gets tough, but take care what you use it on: fuchsias will drop their leaves if sprayed with it.

- Grow lots of moss-curled parsley. Not only is it an invaluable culinary herb, it is also a favourite nesting site for aphids. The cunning ladybird knows this and often lays her eggs in the foliage so that when the larvae hatch out there will be a plentiful supply of aphids to dine on. Neil uses this to his advantage by collecting the larvae in mild weather and placing them among the pots in the glasshouse. 'They are brilliant at curbing aphids early in the season when temperatures are too low to introduce biological controls,' he says.

- Try to find room for some Californian poppies or tagetes in the greenhouse as they are a natural magnet for beneficial insects such as hoverflies and lacewings.

- It may sound anathema to all the principles of organic gardening, but if you want to create a new bed from a turfed area, spray it with glyphosate weedkiller first, advises Neil. This will preserve the topmost mantle of soil that is richest in soil flora and fauna – removing it entirely or burying it too deeply when digging only kills this precious layer. At Clumber the grass was sprayed off first and the surface lightly rotovated, thereby keeping the soil micro-organisms, encouraging earthworms and retaining the fibre that the plants love. For those not wishing to use herbicides, cover the area with black polythene to exclude all light and leave down for at least a year.

When rotted down, turves stacked in layers provide a valuable source of loam.

- If you decide to remove the turf, do not throw it away; it is a valuable source of loam and an ideal substrate for incorporating when you plant fruit trees. Simply stack it upside-down in layers. For every 30cm (12in) of turf, apply a generous layer of manure, about 23cm (9in) thick to act as an accelerator.

- When building up a compost heap, add a layer of manure every 30cm (12in) to accelerate the decomposition process and enrich the resulting compost. 'At Clumber we mulch the borders with garden compost in late spring, that way the plants reap the benefits throughout the growing season. If you apply it in autumn the nutrients are leached out of our sandy soil during the winter months,' explains Neil.

- Do not use leafmould in vegetable beds because it is full of pests such as millipedes and slugs, keep it as a mulch for flower borders instead. However, if you can sterilise it, it is a valuable ingredient in potting mixes to replace peat.

- Wood ash is a valuable source of potash. Collect it before it rains, as the goodness is quickly washed away, and keep it in an airtight container until required.

Chapter 3

Moving Towards Organic Gardening

Tintinhull House Garden, Somerset

With concern for the environment becoming more embedded in everyday consciousness, the sensible gardener is the one who tries out greener methods now before he is compelled to employ them. At Tintinhull House Garden in Somerset, Floyd Summerhayes is embracing just that approach. Not only is he experimenting with ways to conserve water, and adopting novel methods of dealing with slugs and snails, but he is also gradually working out which organic composts and fertilisers work best at Tintinhull. As Floyd explains, close observation will help you learn to select plants that make the most of your garden's natural assets, and bring about its gradual transformation.

History of the garden

Area: 0·8 hectares (2 acres)
Soil: neutral/loam over marl clay
Altitude: 30m (100ft)
Average rainfall: 762mm (30in)
Average winter climate: moderate

The garden at Tintinhull House in Somerset merits several return visits to do it justice. It may only cover 0·8 hectares (2 acres), but it is such a source of inspiration that both experienced and novice gardeners alike will be punch-drunk on plants and reeling with ideas when they leave. In plan, the design of the garden follows strong east-west and north-south axes, and is masterfully sub-divided by tall yew hedges and high brick walls into six separate enclosures, each with its own distinct character. But what sets Tintinhull apart from others in the same great English garden tradition are the exciting planting schemes within this bold formal framework: hot, strident yellows, oranges and reds in one border opposite a much cooler one containing blues, mauves and pinks; brilliant whites thrown into sharp relief against emerald yew hedges; and a smouldering composition of bronze-red foliage with deep red, blue and purple flowers.

The garden was largely the inspiration of Phyllis Reiss, who, with her husband, bought the property in 1933. As most of the rooms in the house overlooked it, her main aim in the garden was to create year-round interest and beauty. When she died in 1961, the National Trust took over the management of the garden. It is thanks to its work and the sensitivity of successive tenants, including leading garden designer and writer Penelope Hobhouse, that the garden has retained so much of its original character and atmosphere more than a generation later.

Floyd's background

Floyd Summerhayes is the man lucky enough to be Head Gardener at Tintinhull, although he is the first to admit that when he came for his interview as assistant to Penelope Hobhouse, he was less than enamoured by the place. 'It was a terrible, damp, foggy morning in March 1992,' he recalls, 'and the garden seemed very grey and dull. But I knew if I didn't take the opportunity, it could be years before a similar job came up in the Trust.' Fortunately any misgivings he may have had about leaving Nymans, where he previously worked, soon melted away. 'Once you get involved in a place like Tintinhull it doesn't take long before you become totally absorbed by it.'

His promotion to Gardener-in-Charge came in 1993, when Penelope and her husband left the property. Like Mrs Reiss and Penelope Hobhouse before him, Floyd is not afraid to try out new planting schemes, and positively revels in finding new gardening techniques.

'I love experimenting. If it works, it is then adopted as standard practice,' he says enthusiastically.

Green gardening at Tintinhull House

Although Tintinhull cannot be termed completely organic, it is certainly a long way down the line. 'I think eventually public demand is going to force organic gardening on the Trust. The sensible gardeners are those who are finding out now what works and what doesn't before they are compelled to do so,' declares Floyd. 'Here we could do away with chemicals entirely, but the Trust would have to do some of the groundwork in terms of educating the visitors; for a year or two they would probably see a drop in standards until pests and predators have built up their own levels.' He admits that leaf diseases are more of a problem to deal with. 'You can match insect with insect but it's slightly different with diseases, as there is no natural predator. Also many older cultivars are less disease-resistant. Do we risk losing these historic plants or must we just resign ourselves to the fact that we need to spray them to ensure their survival?' he asks.

Taking the green route

Floyd confesses that he finds the terminology confusing. 'Labelling on organic products is a minefield. What does organic actually mean? After all, peat is organic in origin but its use is now frowned upon.' For this reason he chooses products only if they have been approved by the Soil Association.

- **Composts**

In line with his desire to hone down the organic practices that actually work at Tintinhull, Floyd finds the best course of action is to concentrate on one subject at a time. 'We tried coir for two years as an alternative to peat in our composts (see also pp.86–8). For us, it didn't work, but that's not to say it is useless, it just didn't suit our method of doing things,' he explains. He has also tried 'Moorland Gold', a product that comprises of recycled, rather than mined peat, which occurs as a by-product of the water industry in the Pennine area.

At present, he makes up two composts of his own. The first is ideal for pots and containers with summer displays:

2 buckets garden soil
2 buckets coir or leafmould
225g (8oz) seaweed meal
125g (4oz) bonemeal
75g (3oz) hoof and horn
50g (2oz) calcified seaweed

The second is superb for tomatoes or greedy feeders in pots:

3 buckets loam
1 bucket well-rotted manure or mushroom compost
1 bucket leafmould

• Fertilisers

Last year he turned his attention to fertilisers. For planting trees and shrubs as well as top-dressing the borders in the ornamental and vegetable garden he uses pelleted chicken manure (incidentally from non-battery farmed hens), which releases its nutrients slowly over time. 'It is the only food the trees and shrubs get and I have found it very good. The secret is to do it every spring to build up soil fertility,' he says. The lawns, on the other hand, are treated to a solution of seaweed extract, which is watered on once a month, excluding January and February. 'It is more labour intensive because you have to apply it so frequently but the results are well worth it because it is like a magic elixir which stimulates growth and gets the worms going,' he enthuses.

- **A change in attitude**

Floyd's desire to take a more environmental approach has meant a certain leap of faith. 'We no longer shroud the plants in a blanket of chemicals, but look at them more closely and treat them only if they need it. It's a question of getting to know your own garden. For instance here we know the old irises have to be sprayed against leaf spot, but *Iris pallida*, that grows alongside them, never seems as susceptible, so we don't bother spraying it.' It is the same with the roses. For example, *Rosa pimpinellifolia* and its cultivars appear problem-free, while others like 'Zéphirine Drouhin' are martyrs to blackspot and mildew, and must be sprayed. 'At home I don't spray at all. The first set of leaves get black spot and fall off, but the second flush is never so badly affected. It's really a cosmetic thing. If the public could accept defoliated roses we wouldn't need to spray but people are constantly told by gardening programmes, magazines and books that we must have pristine gardens,' he says.

Water conservation

Although we rarely run short of water in the British Isles, it should still be regarded as a precious commodity and one to be saved rather than wasted. Also with metering now becoming the norm, it makes financial sense to cut down on our water consumption. At Tintinhull Floyd reckons he has more or less halved the water bill using the following methods:

- **With porous pipe**

Porous pipe has been laid below the soil surface in the borders so that water goes right where it is needed, with less lost through evaporation and run-off. Buried in straight runs, about 15cm (6in) deep, Floyd admits it still presents a problem when herbaceous plants have to be dug up and divided. 'We've found that using a spade at a parallel angle is best because if you do hit it, it tends to glance off.

If you hit it at right angles, you are more inclined to chop straight through it. Although easy to repair, it is a lot of hassle,' he warns.

- **Saving rainwater**

This has proved tremendously successful, but originally started more by accident. 'We were having some gravel delivered and on the lorry was a 550 gallon plastic central heating oil tank, which I bought very cheaply. We plugged it into the guttering on the potting sheds, and were amazed at how quickly it filled up with water. We worked out that from one average roof you could get three to four thousand gallons in just one winter. It almost became an obsession with us, as to how much rainwater it had collected,' he laughs.

It seemed such a sensible idea to harness the rain that there is now a network of eight tanks in place, which supplies the nursery with all its water for the entire year. But typical of Floyd, he wanted to take it a stage further by automating it. 'Water has that wonderful way of finding its own level. The nursery is on a slope so by linking them with pipes and putting in modern ball cock valves you can shut tanks on and off to avoid them overflowing. They then don't need mains water pressure behind them to operate because they are all fed by gravity. We only use a pump in the summer when the level in the main tank starts to go down. I'm certain that with a bit of ingenuity we could make the whole garden completely free of mains water. We've certainly got enough roof area here, but the big problem is where to store the tanks because they are so big and unsightly. On the nursery we looked into buying a modern septic tank to use as an underground reservoir, but it was just too expensive.'

- **Improving the soil with organic matter**

Organic matter has a curious habit of both increasing the moisture-holding qualities of sandy soils as well as improving the drainage qualities of clay soils. 'If you apply enough organic matter, your plants are far less likely to run short of water. Mulching also helps to prevent evaporation from the soil surface,' says Floyd.

- **Choosing the right plants**

All plants need water for healthy growth, but some are better adapted to surviving droughts than others. Those with fleshy, tiny or silver-grey leaves (xerophytes) will revel in dry situations. 'Get to know your garden and its microclimates, and choose plants that will suit the conditions,' Floyd advises. You will be far more successful if you work with nature rather than fight it.

Water conservation and containers

Always opt for the largest containers you can accommodate because they will lose water more slowly than small ones. Floyd prefers loam-based to peat-based composts as they are more moisture-retentive and promote tighter, more resilient growth (see p.50 for his recipe for container compost). He also advises against cramming in too many plants because this does not leave enough space for roots to develop. 'The containers are only watered twice a week, usually Mondays and Fridays. If we have to do it more frequently than that, we have selected the wrong plants.'

Making garden compost

Like all good gardeners, Floyd realises the soil is a dynamic, living thing, and one which should be respected. 'The difference with organic gardeners is that they put all their energies into feeding the soil and as a result the plants get looked after,' he explains. The soil at Tintinhull has been gardened well for many years and mostly comprises of fertile loam overlying marl clay. However, that is not to say Floyd ever rests on his laurels for he is always striving to improve it with organic matter. He favours spent mushroom compost for the flower borders because it is cheap, sterile and lightweight. However, due to its high lime content it has a tendency to raise the pH of the soil. To counteract this Floyd composts it separately to allow the lime to wash through and improve its straw-like appearance. After about six months the metamorphosis is complete and Floyd is rewarded with a rich dark crumbly substance that is a joy to spread and also sets off the plants beautifully when used as a mulch.

The soil in the vegetable beds is replenished annually with garden compost, which is made in a vast compost bin measuring about 8m (25ft) long by 2·5m (8ft) wide by 1·2m (4ft) high. There are three such containers, each one being built to hold a year's waste. 'It may sound like a funny *ad hoc* system but we just dump the rubbish inside until it is about knee height, or until we physically cannot get in there any longer. When that happens we periodically stack it properly at the far end. This mixes the contents, and because there is a large volume of compost, it heats up to kill weed seeds. When full, it is covered with a plastic sheet and left for up to two years,' Floyd explains.

Any material that can be composted is composted. Woody garden prunings are chopped up first using a new generation 'quiet' shredder. As its name implies, it is much easier on the ears, and contains within it a small wheel with serrated teeth that crushes up the material. The shreddings are still fairly coarse but the machine works well whether they are wet or dry. 'If the wood is too large to go through the shredder, I will either burn it here or take it home for turning. The shavings then come back to the compost heap,' he says.

Worm bins

Floyd runs his own garden at home completely following organic principles, largely because of his young family but also because he is not required to please anybody but himself. 'There I am free to try out different methods without public pressure,' he declares.

In recent years he has been converted to worm bins as a way of disposing of kitchen waste. 'I wouldn't be without them now. Not only do you get rich dark compost, you also get free liquid fertiliser in the process. (This should be diluted at a rate of 1 part liquid to 10 of water). The worms are a bit like pets because you have to feed and look after them, and the kids love them,' he laughs. The special dark red worms, known as 'brandling' or 'tiger' worms, can only cope with small quantities of scraps, so Floyd has two worm bins to ensure neither becomes overloaded.

His favourite and most successful bin comprises of a stack of three trays. When it becomes full, the bottom layer is removed and emptied, then placed on top of the other two. The cycle then starts again. 'I have found it an excellent system,' enthuses Floyd. If you fancy the idea of a worm compost, you do not necessarily need to splash out on a purpose-built bin; a modified dustbin, water butt or similar plastic container can work just as well (see illustration).

- If the bin does not have a tap, drill twenty or thirty 10mm (½in) drainage holes at the base to remove excess liquid.

- Drill fifteen 10mm (½in) holes at the top for ventilation.

Cross section of the layers in a worm bin showing the ventilation holes and tight-fitting lid.

Emptying the worm bin. Worms will congregate under damp newspaper, and can be used to set up a new bin.

- First add a layer of coarse sand or gravel to a depth of 10cm (4in) to keep drainage holes clear and support the divider.

- Cut to shape and insert a divider, made of wood or old carpet. Add a few holes to allow the liquid to drain through.

- Add about 8cm (3in) of bedding material, complete with worms, preferably taken from an existing compost heap. You need at least one hundred worms, but if you can get more, so much the better.

- After about a week start adding kitchen waste. This could be anything from fruit and vegetable peelings to bread, rice, pasta, tea bags, coffee grounds and egg shells.

- Keep the food scraps covered with damp newspaper at all times to discourage fruit flies and ensure worms stay moist.

- Cover with a tight-fitting lid to shed rain.

- Add kitchen waste gradually; it should never be more than 5cm (2in) thick. When this is well colonised with worms you can add more.

- When the bin is full, spread out the contents onto a large sheet of plastic in the sun. To coax the worms from the compost, place damp newspaper over it and wait; the worms, preferring moist dark conditions, will congregate there, and can be used to set up a new bin.

What can go wrong with worm bins

- Unpleasant smells and dead worms could either indicate a lack of ventilation or an over abundance of waste, which the worms cannot process quickly enough. To remedy this stop adding food and improve the conditions inside the bin by mixing up its contents with shredded newspaper to soak up excess moisture.

- An infestation of small black fruit flies often accompanies worm bins as they are attracted by the smell of rotting fruit and vegetables. Ensure the waste is kept covered with damp newspaper and reduce their numbers by trapping them with yellow sticky cards inside the bin, or even sucking them up in a vacuum cleaner!

- The contents of worm bins often become acidic. Remedy with a handful of ground limestone or dolomite limestone every month. Try not to add large quantities of citrus peel.

Wildlife at Tintinhull

One of the most obvious changes at Tintinhull in recent years is the increased presence of birds, particularly blue tits and thrushes, which help to control aphids and snails respectively. This may be down to the fact that the garden no longer has a feline patrol, but it could also be due to decreased use of chemicals. It also coincides with the Trust's improvement of the surrounding habitats; the adjacent orchard and boundary hedgerows are both being renewed and enriched, thereby increasing the shelter and food supply for wildlife occupants.

Within the garden itself Floyd has been steadily adding to the nest boxes that already exist. Following RSPB recommendations, he makes them himself from off-cuts of timber used elsewhere. His assistant, Tanis, is particularly keen on birds and keeps a daily record of those she has seen in the garden. The list makes gratifying reading: woodpeckers, tree creepers, fieldfares, mistle thrushes, sparrow

Verbena bonariensis

hawks and buzzards; Floyd has even spotted a kingfisher over the long pool.

Insects also abound. Wasps are particularly numerous; Floyd feels they have more of an effect on the aphid population than ladybirds, especially later in the season. 'The secret is to get as much diversity in the garden as possible, which has got to help somewhere down the line,' he says. The borders are jam-packed; throughout the year there is always something in flower. Notable wildlife magnets are foxgloves, *Nepeta* 'Six Hills Giant', buddlejas, *Verbena bonariensis*, and sedum (see pp.19-20, 115-16 and 128-9). He even lets a few parsnips go to seed in the vegetable garden to attract hoverflies and other insects. 'It produces a stunning, large, yellow cow parsley-like flower. Growing narrow and tall up to about 2·5m (8ft), it's great for the back of the border. A real talking point,' Floyd assures.

Slugs and snails

In recent years Floyd has substantially reduced his use of slug pellets to control slugs and snails, preferring instead to let the increased numbers of songbirds do the job for him. 'Rather than sprinkling pellets around everywhere, I am now targeting plants such as delphiniums and *Campanula lactiflora*, that I know struggle. Also we now grow many more hostas in pots where they are less prone to attack,' he explains.

In the past he has tried various means of deterring the slimy miscreants. One included sprinkling baked, crushed eggshells thickly around susceptible plants, which was moderately successful, but required more shells than he was able to save. After all, there is a limit to how many eggs one can reasonably consume! The other, more novel approach, was to use electricity. 'I used to grow alpines and dwarf bulbs in cold frames. To keep out slugs and snails I put two copper wires about an inch apart, and linked to a torch battery, round the top of the frame. If anything crossed the two wires it would create a circuit and electrocute them. It was a bit of a palaver, but it worked!' he laughs.

Sprinkling baked crushed eggshells around young hosta shoots to discourage slugs.

Tips

- Standing plants outside during the hottest months of the summer will significantly reduce pest and disease problems in the greenhouse. Floyd grows tomatoes tied to bamboo canes in large pots for this very reason (see p.50 for his compost recipe for tomatoes). Not only do they have more root space than in a cumbersome grow bag, it also makes them far more mobile.

A simple container made from four wooden posts hammered into the ground and surrounded by flexible sheep netting is ideal for leafmould.

- Collect autumn leaves on the lawn with a mower. This is quicker than raking them up by hand and also chops them into smaller pieces, which helps speed up the decomposition process. The inclusion of grass seems to make little difference to the end result.

- Fish eat frog and toad spawn. If you want both, consider having two ponds in the garden: one with fish and one without.

- Leave the top growth on herbaceous plants for as long as possible to provide seeds, nesting sites and shelter for wildlife. Unless the borders are earmarked for bulbs in the autumn, Floyd will cut down plants only when they turn black and unsightly. Otherwise they remain intact until the end of February.

- Use flexible sheep netting to hold in leaves when making leafmould.

- Don't be over zealous when tidying the garden; pile up some undiseased wood in an undisturbed corner to create further habitats for wildlife.

Chapter 4

Companion Planting

Hill Top, Cumbria

Fascinatingly, the increasing popularity of organic gardening has revived interest in the methods used to control pests in the past. When planted close to each other, it was observed that certain plants, such as onions and carrots, appeared to benefit their neighbours by confusing pests with their stronger scent. Although you might be tempted to dismiss old wives' tales, many myths are founded on reality from a time when farmers and gardeners were perhaps more in tune with their crops. The mixed plantings maintained by Peter Tasker at Hill Top in Cumbria are just as effective: showy, scented flowers can attract beneficial insects that keep pests at bay, and help contribute to a balanced ecological environment.

History of the garden

Area: 0·2 hectares (½ acre)
Soil: acid/loam
Altitude: 90m (295ft)
Average rainfall: 1,524mm (60in)
Average winter climate: moderate

Rolling green fells, ribboned with criss-crossing dry-stone walls, interspersed with huge mirror-like lakes, characterises the immediate landscape around Hill Top. The dour, dark grey pebble-dashed farmhouse looks somewhat unprepossessing but its charm did not escape Beatrix Potter, who purchased the property with the proceeds of her book *The Tale of Peter Rabbit* when she was nearly 40. She married a local solicitor and lived in a nearby house, but still used Hill Top as a studio, and drew much inspiration from the house and garden when writing and illustrating her books.

She was a great supporter and benefactor of the National Trust and when she died in 1943 she left instructions that Hill Top, the farm, and over 1,618 hectares (4,000 acres) of pasture and fell should pass to the organisation after her husband's death. Although little information about the garden exists, its design and content are loosely based on old photographs, journal notes and Beatrix Potter's own illustrations. Anyone familiar with *The Tale of Jemima Puddle-Duck* will recognise the green gate to the vegetable garden and the rhubarb patch in which Jemima Puddle-Duck tries to conceal her eggs. Or the little white gate in the wall on which Tom Kitten sat and watched the Puddle-Duck family waddle past.

Around 70,000 people a year visit the house and garden. So popular is it as a tourist attraction that the new entrance building at the bottom of the garden rarely empties at the height of the season. This success is a double-edged sword as it puts a great deal of pressure on the house which is why a timed ticket system has been introduced to limit visitor numbers at any given time.

Pete's background

Following a three-year stint working at the Royal Botanic Gardens in Kew, Pete Tasker was taken on by the Trust in 1988 as a 'peripatetic' gardener. This curious title meant he was to take charge of several gardens in the area since many were too small to justify the employment of a full-time member of staff. Hill Top, Townend's cottage plot and the town garden at Wordsworth House were those designated upon his arrival, with the addition of Stagshaw's rhododendron woodland and the Victorian garden at High Close later on.

Presently his main focus of attention will once again be Hill Top and High Close, with occasional visits to Wordsworth House in Cockermouth. 'I like my job because it's so varied and because I have a certain amount of freedom to decide what I do when. The gardens are all so different. I like working at High Close because as a new project, there is much developmental work to be undertaken, it's not solely a question of maintenance, but Hill Top is probably my favourite because it feels like home,' he says.

In the past Pete would spend just the morning at Hill Top, ensuring he completed his tasks before 11am when the property opened. 'The Trust likes you to be on site to answer questions but if you are not careful you don't do anything else! One of the perils of being a National Trust gardener is that people expect you to know everything about your own garden and everything about everyone else's too. I've even been asked about houseplants!'

That said, he admits to enjoying the interaction with visitors, even though he has lost count of the number of times he has been asked if he is Mr McGregor, the fierce old gardener with a white beard who used to chase Peter Rabbit with a rake. 'Actually a rabbit did get through into the vegetable garden and caused quite a bit of damage. I ended up chasing it out – just like Mr McGregor, in fact. It was quite surreal catching myself doing that!' laughs Pete.

A miscellany of flowers, fruit and vegetables

Covering only about 0·2 hectares (½ acre), the garden at Hill Top is on an intimate, accessible scale, maintained in the style of a traditional cottage plot. Orderly rows of vegetables and fruit give way to a mixed planting of bulbs, annuals, perennials and flowering shrubs. Old-fashioned favourites like campanulas, delphiniums, hardy geraniums, lupins and phlox grow cheek by jowl with viburnums, lilacs and spiraeas. But surprising chords of sophistication are struck by the white wisteria shining out against the dark of the farmhouse, and *Eucryphia glutinosa*, whose white flowers are a magnet for insects in July and August.

A second area beyond a dry-stone wall is devoted mainly to the cultivation of fruit and vegetables, but even here self-sown opportunists such as verbascum, alchemilla and honesty are allowed to flourish as a happy jumble. 'We've cheated a bit because we've set this up as a mini Mr McGregor's garden, although no one is sure where his garden was actually located,' Pete explains. A carefully placed antiquated riddle, spade, watering can and some clay pots help to lend an air of authenticity to the scene.

As the garden is primarily a show-piece, vegetables are selected more for their appearance than flavour. Pete regularly grows the dramatic scarlet-stemmed ruby chard, red frilly-leaved lettuce and 'Painted Lady' runner beans, whose vermilion and white flowers rival those of any conventional climber. 'I also went through a stage of growing unusual potatoes like the knobbly 'Pink Fir Apple' and blue-fleshed 'Edzell Blue.' I like to leave the spuds in as long as possible to show visitors what they are like. It's surprising how many children have never seen potatoes growing. One child even asked me if the rhubarb was real because he'd never seen the plant before.'

Fruit is also well catered for at Hill Top. Morello cherries hug the north-facing wall while blackcurrants, white currants, gooseberries, raspberries and a strawberry patch bask in the sun. Most years there is normally more than enough fruit and vegetables even after the birds have had their fill. As there is no restaurant on the premises, Pete shares out the produce from the garden with the staff in the house and shop before taking the rest home. 'It's a bit like being paid to have an allotment. I really missed it when I didn't work here for a while,' he laughs.

Companion planting at Hill Top

Companion planting may be steeped in folklore and old wives' tales, but in the days before weedkillers and pesticides were invented, farmers and gardeners, who were probably much more in tune with their crops, noticed that certain plants had an effect on neighbouring species. Some improved the health and vigour of nearby plants, while others had the opposite effect and suppressed growth. Companion planting seems to work in a number of ways:

The poached egg plant,
Limnanthes douglasii

- attracting beneficial insects. The colourful yellow and white poached egg plant, *Limnanthes douglasii*, orange Californian poppy, *Eschscholzia californica*, and lavender blue *Phacelia tanacetifolia* are all excellent at luring beneficial insects which then attack pests such as aphids.

- repelling pests through smell. Planting onions around carrots is thought to confuse the carrot root fly, likewise French marigolds planted just outside the greenhouse are said to discourage whitefly from entering. Herbs with aromatic oils such as rosemary, thyme and hyssop will mask the scent of maturing brassicas, thereby discouraging the cabbage white butterfly from homing in and laying their eggs.

French marigolds planted just outside the greenhouse door will discourage whitefly from entering.

The nodules on the roots of clover help to fix nitrogen in the air and make it available to plants in the soil.

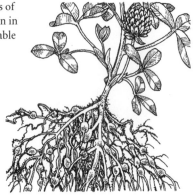

- deterring plant growth through root secretions. For example, the potato cyst eelworm is said to be discouraged by the secretions from French marigold roots.

- adding soil fertility. Plants in the legume family like lupin and clover are able to fix nitrogen in nodules on their roots, which can then be used by other crops.

At Hill Top all types of plants jostle for attention. Such a rich diversity attracts a wide range of wildlife, which in theory makes for a stable ecology because no one pest or disease becomes dominant. 'Companion planting happens more by accident really. I don't think anyone made a conscious decision to grow things this way. We grow vegetables but we try to make the effect more ornamental by planting blocks of flowers in between. My favourites include feverfew, pot marigolds and opium poppies. I also use herbs such as parsley in a similar way. Sometimes I leave a row of leeks just for their beautiful spherical mauve flowerheads, which many insects love. In a small garden like this I seriously doubt whether it makes that much difference between putting flowers right next to the vegetables or planting them ten yards away. But the flowers definitely attract beneficial insects,' says Pete.

Self-seeders

'Unmanicured' is how Pete describes the garden at Hill Top. For practical and historical reasons the fruit and vegetables are grown in neat rows but flowering plants are positively encouraged to self-sow to soften straight lines and heighten the impression of natural profusion. Notorious space invaders include honesty, verbascum, alchemilla, foxgloves and golden feverfew which are allowed to self-sow at will unless the area has been ear-marked for something more important. These prolific colonisers often have an uncanny knack of choosing just the right spot in which to grow and looking far better than if they had been planned.

Many colourful hardy annuals share this natural proclivity to self-sow, and as such will continue to pop up year after year with little intervention. To establish them in the first place, in April or May simply clear an area of ground and rake it to form a fine tilth. Broadcast the seed evenly or sow it in shallow drills (a). Lightly rake over the surface to ensure most of the seeds will be lightly covered with soil. Water well in dry weather and thin out overcrowded groups of seedlings (b). Some of Pete's favourites at Hill Top are described below, including their value to wildlife:

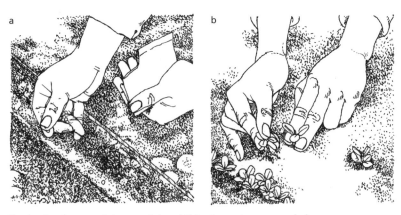

Sowing hardy annuals in rows (a) and thinning out over crowded groups of seedings (b).

Calendula officinalis (**pot marigold**) Orange, yellow or apricot daisy-like flowerheads produced well into autumn; 30–70cm (12–28in) tall; attractive to bees, hoverflies and butterflies.

Clarkia unguiculata (**syn. *C. elegans***) Funnel-shaped, satin-like flowers in a range of colours from mauve and pink to reddish-purple; 30–90cm (12–36in) tall; attractive to bees and a source of food for caterpillars.

Limnanthes douglasii (**poached egg plant**) Saucer-shaped yellow and white flowers; 15cm (6in) tall; attractive to bees, hoverflies and butterflies.

Nigella damascena (**love-in-a-mist**) Blue, white or pink semi-double flowers often surrounded by a ruff of feathery foliage, followed by inflated seed heads; 50cm (20in) tall; attractive to bees and butterflies.

Papaver somniferum (**opium poppy**) Bowl-shaped, tissue-like flowers in shades of pink, mauve, red and white, followed by large, blue-green seed pods; to 1·2m (4ft) tall; attracts hoverflies and bees.

Reseda odorata (**mignonette**) Sweetly-scented though insignificant yellow-green flowerheads; 30cm (12in) tall; source of nectar for butterflies.

Mignonette, *Reseda odorata*

Tropaeolum majus (**nasturtium**) Orange, red or yellow long-spurred flowers and kidney-shaped light green leaves; will climb up or spread along the ground to a length of 3m (10ft) or so; caterpillar food plant and beloved by hoverflies.

Disease-resistant roses

Screening the garden from the apple and damson orchard is a rustic wooden trellis, topped with charming goose egg finials and enveloped with climbing and rambler roses. In high summer it comes alive with insects: ladybirds and hoverflies are drawn by the promise of aphids, and bees buzz from flower to flower in drunken raptures. Comprising mostly of old cultivars such as the purplish-pink 'Madame Isaac Pereire' and pale pink 'Fantin-Latour', the roses are prone to the tiresome trio of blackspot, rust and mildew, to which Pete now turns a blind eye. 'I used to spray with a cocktail of chemicals for greenfly and blackspot but it was never that successful. Then one year I decided not to spray as an experiment; the greenfly came and went, the blackspot was a bit worse, but on balance there was very little difference. And it was obviously a lot easier for me.'

Although none can ever be cited as completely bombproof as they may succumb in some areas or in particularly bad years, the list of disease-resistant rose cultivars is growing. Should Pete ever want to dig out his most disease-prone climbers and ramblers, the following have been shown to have a robust constitution:

'Bantry Bay' Upright, cluster-flowered climber with deep pink, lightly scented flowers; 4m (12ft) tall.

'Compassion' Upright, large-flowered climber with pink, shaded apricot, very fragrant flowers; 3m (10ft) tall.

'Dortmund' Upright, cluster-flowered climber with single red blooms with a white eye, borne freely from summer to autumn; 3m (10ft) tall.

'Dublin Bay' Freely branching climber with deep red double flowers, produced from summer to autumn; 2·2m (7ft) tall.

'Golden Showers' Stiff, upright climber with double, golden yellow, fragrant flowers from summer to autumn; 3m (10ft) tall.

'Maigold' Stiff-growing climber with semi-double, fragrant, bronze-yellow flowers in early summer, then sparsely in autumn; 2·5m (8ft) tall.

'New Dawn' Rambler with clusters of shell pink, fragrant flowers from summer to autumn; tolerates a partially shaded site; 3m (10ft) tall.

'Rosy Mantle' Stiff climber with deep pink, fragrant flowers, produced from summer to autumn; 2·5m (8ft) tall.

'Super Elfin' Rambler with geranium red flowers with little fragrance; 3m (10ft) tall.

Chemicals

Pete now only uses chemicals when he has to. 'I attended a nationally recognised chemical application course, along with other Trust gardeners, in which we learnt about applying pesticides and herbicides, as well as mixing, calibrating, disposal and cleaning techniques. It all seemed like such a palaver that most of us have never done any spraying since because it is just not worth the bother. I think we were all guilty of using them too much in the past, so the new legislation is a good thing, not only from a health and safety point of view but also from an environmental standpoint,' Pete declares.

The only concession he makes is glyphosate, which he sprays on to kill deep rooting perennial weeds such as bindweed (see p.97). 'We do have patches of ground elder and couch grass, but I prefer to dig that out,' he says. He is also a great believer in the hoe. Carried out regularly, hoeing keeps many annual weeds such as the sticky goosegrass (*Galium aparine*) under control.

Slugs and snails

Enjoying or suffering from (depending on your outlook) 1,524mm (60in) annual rainfall, the garden rarely gets a sniff of drought. This, coupled with the abundance of dry-stone walls where they hide, means that Hill Top is Utopia for slugs and snails. 'They are a real pain,' Pete affirms. 'In the past I have used slug pellets but it was never popular with visitors who would often comment on the threat they posed to birds and other wildlife. In future they will have to put up with a few tatty leaves as I give up using slug pellets. It's only because we have all been conditioned to seeing immaculate gardens with perfect foliage and not a weed in sight, that we think that's how they should be.'

This year by way of experimentation he is abandoning pellets in favour of pinhead oatmeal, a tip he gleaned from Andrew Sawyer, Head Gardener at Cragside in Northumberland, who uses it with tremendous success around dahlias. According to Pete its benefits are double-edged. Firstly, slugs and snails are rather partial to it, preferring it to the plant it surrounds. Secondly, it appeals to the gastronomic tastes of many birds, that eat it as an appetiser before the main course of slug.

'Someone also told me that crushed up potato crisps were quite effective. Maybe they can't stop themselves from eating them and the salt makes them horribly dehydrated in the morning!' jokes Pete. On a more serious note, he reckons that picking them off on a wet night is as good a control as any, as well as attracting their natural predators such as hedgehogs, frogs, toads, newts and birds.

Tips

- In a cottage garden use hazel sticks for bean poles rather than bamboo as they look perfect in this setting. They last about two years before becoming brittle.

- Have a bonfire to burn perennial weeds, diseased material or anything that is too big to compost. 'There is nothing quite like it in the autumn to get rid of rubbish. As long as the material is dry enough to burn quickly at a high temperature and it is only done occasionally, say twice a year, it will not contribute much to the greenhouse effect,' thinks Pete.

- Don't try to rake out all the stones if your soil is inherently stony, as at Hill Top, because more will wash through to the surface. 'I tried this for years and it never got any better. Now I simply leave them alone because they actually make quite a good mulch and stop plants drying out in the summer,' he says.

- Make sure you do not accidentally introduce pernicious weeds such as bindweed to your garden when you take delivery of manure. Once they take hold around established plants, they are very difficult to eradicate even with glyphosate weedkiller.

Chapter 5

Urban Organic Gardening

Fenton House, London

There is little doubt that a tiny plot marooned in a sea of concrete, with the noise and pollution that such a site inevitably brings, would struggle to be a successful organic garden because it would not be able to attract the range of beneficial creatures needed to keep pests at bay. Thankfully, few gardens are created in such isolation. The more usual scenario in urban areas is a conglomeration of small plots, which, when viewed as a whole, can have a big impact on wildlife because unlike most of us, birds, reptiles and insects do not recognise legal boundaries and will move freely from one to another. A town·garden like Fenton House in London may not boast the wide range of birds and wildlife more usually associated with the countryside, but, as Danny Snapes says, with thoughtful plant selection and the creation of suitable habitats, any creatures that are present will be encouraged to stay, even in a tiny plot.

History of the garden

Area: 0·6 hectares (1½ acres)
Soil: neutral/sandy loam
Altitude: 122m (400ft)
Average rainfall: 635mm (25in)
Average winter climate: moderate

Should the frenetic pace of life in London leave you feeling more than a little jaded, a pit stop at Fenton House could be just the antidote you need to recharge your batteries. Located in the well-heeled suburb of Hampstead, it may only be a mile or so from the capital's centre, but its atmosphere couldn't feel more different. The constant low drone of the traffic outside the boundary walls aside, you could almost be transported back to the late seventeenth century when the property enjoyed a village setting.

Although the National Trust acquired Fenton House in 1953, it was not until 1982 that a garden more in keeping with the property was created. What visitors can enjoy today is an intimate garden, made all the more appealing because it is on a scale that most of us can identify with. Its design now incorporates a formal evergreen framework softened by relaxed but exuberant planting. The change in levels and visual blocks allow many elements of surprise, the greatest of which must surely be the sight of the lower garden with its orchard, vegetables, cut flowers, herbs and lean-to glasshouse.

Danny's background

Danny Snapes has been Gardener-in-Charge at Fenton House since 1996, but admits he came into horticulture in a round about way. 'For nine years I was employed at John Lewis' in High Wycombe, Hertfordshire, but I knew I needed a change.' On his days off he studied at the local agricultural college, and also worked at Bressingham Plant Centre at Dorney, which was invaluable for gaining plant knowledge. 'I ended up working seven days a week because I also became a volunteer gardener at Cliveden in Buckinghamshire. But it was all worth it because I got the job here at Fenton House, where I'm happier than I have ever been. It's good not to have constant pressure, to be working outside with plants and watching them grow and develop. I also like being in charge and knowing that, within reason, I can try out new things if I want to,' says Danny.

Advantages and disadvantages of an urban site

Covering 0.6 hectares (1½ acres), Fenton House is hardly typical of the average town garden, but despite its size, it has much in common with smaller urban plots. The main pros and cons of town sites are outlined below:

- **Increased warmth**

The chief advantage is increased warmth and shelter afforded by all the buildings, walls and concrete, which adds to the range of plants that can be grown and also extends the growing season by several weeks over that of country areas. 'There is a definite microclimate within the walls of the garden. I reckon it could be as much as 2 to 5°C (36 to 41°F) higher than the outside. We still get frosts, but rarely serious ones. In the last few years plants, such as daffodils, seem to be showing through earlier and earlier,' Danny declares.

He tailors the planting to suit the pH and soil type within the garden, which ranges from slightly acid to alkaline, from predominately Bagshot sand to pockets of London clay. Grey-leaved plants such as artemisia, ballota and perovskia do tremendously well in the hot sunny spots, as do aromatic herbs like rosemary, sage and lavender. 'Just before Easter I cut back the old English lavender hedge. This is later than normally recommended, but it does not seem to affect their growth in any way and also creates an overwintering site for ladybirds into the bargain,' says Danny.

Other shrubs of borderline hardiness that revel in the increased warmth include two members of the pea family: *Coronilla valentina* subsp. *glauca* (syn. *C. glauca*), with sweetly-scented yellow flowers in early spring, and *Indigofera amblyantha*, with pink flowers from summer to early autumn. Unsurprisingly, tender wall shrubs also flourish here at Fenton; two of the most successful are the delightful yellow *Rosa banksiae* 'Lutea' and the fragrant *Jasminum officinale*.

- **Cost and availability of organic matter**

With the exception of noise and pollution, locating a source of good, cheap organic matter is probably the single biggest disadvantage in urban areas. 'It's a nightmare to get compost and manure in London, and when you do find it, it costs a fortune,' bemoans Danny. 'If I wanted to mulch all the borders with horse muck, I would have to spend about £3000 per year!' As a cheaper option, he goes for mushroom compost, which is easier to obtain, lightweight

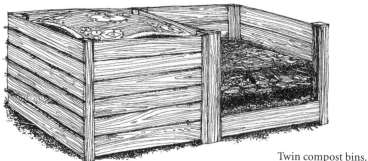

Twin compost bins.
The heap is built up in layers and covered
with a piece of carpet to retain the heat.

and comes conveniently bagged up (look in Yellow Pages under 'Mushroom Growers'). Due to its high alkaline content, Danny refrains from using it too often; once every two or three years is enough to improve the borders without radically altering their pH.

The importance of organic matter to keep the soil in good heart and the difficulty in obtaining enough of it, makes it even more vital for Danny to make his own compost. At present he has six bins, each one measuring 1·2m long (4ft) × 1m (3ft) wide × 1·2m (4ft) high, at various stages of decay. He builds up the heap in layers so that no one material ever dominates. Perennial weeds, diseased material and plants with woody growth are not composted, but nothing else is wasted: grass clippings, annual weeds, soil, shredded prunings and kitchen waste from his own home all end up on the compost heap, which is kept covered with a plastic sheet and carpet to retain the heat. Within six to nine months he is rewarded with dark brown, crumbly, high quality compost, ideal as a mulch on the borders.

• Wind turbulence

Although the walls bring increased warmth and protection, they also create problems with wind. 'It comes over the top then vortexes around and breaks things within the garden. Tall herbaceous plants are most at risk and must be properly staked,' says Danny. An added disadvantage of a totally walled-in garden is that disease spores become trapped within and are less likely to be blown away.

Green gardening at Fenton House

At Fenton House Danny is determined to give Nature a helping hand. 'I have always been very keen on organic gardening, and I will not use chemicals if I can help it. My main problem is yarrow in the lawn, which is very difficult to control without spraying,' he says. There is also a host of old-fashioned asters in the top border, which are prone to powdery mildew, particularly when they become over-crowded or run short of water. Taking them out completely is not an option because they are an important part of the planting, but Danny has noticed their health has shown a marked improvement with the installation of an irrigation system. One of the trouble-free members of the tribe is the mauve *Aster × frikartii*. 'It's a superb plant, no problem at all,' he enthuses.

Aster × frikartii

- **Controlling slugs and snails**

  If all else fails, Danny is not averse to completely removing diseased or pest-ridden plants, provided, of course, they are not of historical importance – unique to the property or essential to its character. 'It's just not worth persevering with them. Far better to ditch them and start afresh,' he says. This is exactly what happened to a bed of hostas and ferns, which was meant to look green and restful throughout the summer months. 'It was so ravaged by slugs and snails that it was bringing down the quality of the garden, so it had to go,' says Danny.

'The previous gardener used to apply slug pellets but I've never applied them here. After a while I noticed that a pair of song thrushes had taken up residence in the garden, and they did a good job of controlling snails. I knew this by the number of smashed shells I used to find on the lawn!' he laughs. However, these birds have since disappeared, which Danny puts down to the presence of three new cats at the property. Without his two feathered friends to oblige him, he must be even more vigilant to ensure slugs and snails do not gain the upper hand. 'I make a point of cleaning through the garden on a regular basis, weeding and picking off dead leaves as I go. I am sure good hygiene and husbandry help to prevent problems.' If he does find snails, he cuts short their progress with a deft stamp of his boot.

He is also keen to try out the naturally occurring parasite, *Phasmarhabditis*, to control slugs. This lives in the moisture surrounding soil particles and enters the slug, multiplying inside it and eventually killing it. A swollen 'mantle' on its back indicates the presence of nematodes in a slug, but since it goes underground to die, you may not find any corpses. The beauty (if you can call it) of the parasite is that it is specific to slugs, and occasionally small snails, so is totally harmless to other wildlife.

Millions of nematodes are supplied suspended in clay in a small sachet. When mixed with water, they can be applied to moist soil with a watering can. To be effective the soil temperature must not fall below 5°C (41°F), so the best time for application is usually around mid-April. The treated area is protected for up to six weeks.

• **Attracting birds**

The absence of any worthwhile water feature (in terms of wildlife) means that reptilean predators are thin on the ground, so Danny knows it makes even greater sense to attract birds to the garden. Fortunately its proximity to Hampstead Heath ensures a wide range of visitors, including long-tailed tits, nuthatches, green and greater spotted woodpeckers and even sparrow hawks. 'I recently bought some squirrel-proof (essential in this area) bird feeders and filled them with peanuts and seed. Amazingly, this increased the bird population in the garden by about four times, which I was very pleased about,' says Danny. He also plans to put up nesting and bat boxes in the hope that these creatures will not just drop in occasionally, but will actually make the garden their home.

• Coping with weeds

Blissfully for Danny, pernicious weeds are absent in the borders at Fenton House. 'I count myself lucky because I do not have to worry about bindweed, ground elder or horsetail; the odd dandelion is about as bad as it gets here.' He sets great store by hand weeding, not only does it remove weeds, it aerates the soil and shows off the plants in the borders. Never far from his side when weeding is his prized three-pronged hand cultivator. 'It is such a useful little tool because you can use it to fluff up the soil after you have removed the weeds and it makes such a difference to the look of the borders,' he enthuses.

Weeds in the beds are one thing, those in paths are another matter. With around 1,000 square metres of gravel to contend with, Danny plans to invest in a weed burner, which heats up to 1000°C (1832°F) and scorches off any weeds as well as their seeds in two seconds. 'It is not a cheap option. The model I've been looking at, which is mobile and lightweight to cope with the different levels, would set me back around £700. But in the end I think it will prove cost-effective, and is certainly preferable to applying herbicides,' he says.

A three-pronged hand-cultivator is ideal for fluffing up the soil after weeding.

Evergreen structure

Although predominately a summer garden, the planting at Fenton House is an object lesson in how to bring winter interest to a town plot. Without the distraction of colour and the softening effect of foliage, the clean lines of clipped box and yew hedging together with topiary holly specimens in this formal garden become all the more arresting. Add to this the natural domed contours of evergreen shrubs such as myrtles and osmanthus and a permanent backbone is created, that not only stems the monotony of a bare winter landscape, but also provides unexpected benefits for wildlife in terms of protection, nesting sites and a source of food. Some of the most successful evergreens found at Fenton House are outlined below:

Arbutus unedo (**strawberry tree**) Spreading small tree or large shrub, to 8m (25ft) tall, with red-brown flaky bark. Produces tiny, urn-shaped white flowers in autumn coinciding with the fleshy red 'strawberries' from the previous year's flowers. Birds cannot get enough of them.

Strawberry tree, *Arbutus unedo*

Buxus sempervirens (**common box**) Bushy rounded shrub, to 5m (15ft) tall. Many different foliage forms are available: 'Elegantissima' has white-margined leaves; 'Marginata' has yellow-edged foliage; 'Suffruticosa' is slow-growing, compact and ideal for low hedges.

Fatsia japonica Rounded architectural shrub, to 3m (10ft), with leathery, lobed hand-shaped foliage and drumstick-like brownish flowers in autumn, followed by black fruit.

Ilex aquifolium (**holly**) Pyramidal tree or shrub, to 15m (50ft) tall, that can be clipped into interesting shapes. Both male and female plants are required to obtain berries, which are usually red, and beloved by birds. Many different foliage forms are available: 'Argentea Marginata', a female cultivar that crops freely with white margined leaves; 'J.C. van Tol', a self-fertile female tree with dark green leaves and few spines; *I.* × *altaclerensis* 'Golden King', a compact female form with rounded leaves, margined yellow.

Myrtus communis (**common myrtle**) Bushy shrub, to 3m (10ft) tall, with glossy aromatic foliage. Its white autumn flowers with conspicuous stamens are followed by purple-black berries. Requires a sheltered, sunny site.

Olea europaea (**olive**) Rounded shrub with grey-green foliage and whitish flowers followed by edible round fruit. Requires a sunny, sheltered site and sharply drained soil to survive the British winter. At Fenton House they grow outside all year in pots.

Osmanthus delavayi Rounded, bushy shrub, to 5m (15ft) tall, with finely-toothed dark green foliage and fragrant white flowers from mid- to late spring.

Prunus lusitanica (**Portugal laurel**) Dense bushy shrub or tree, to 12m (40ft) tall, with red-stemmed leaves. Responds well to clipping and shaping. At Fenton House they are grown as standards in tubs to mimic citrus bushes. Scented white flowers are followed by cherry-like fruits, beloved by birds.

Viburnum tinus Compact, bushy shrub, to 3m (10ft) tall, with white winter flowers and blue-black fruit.

Tips

- Protect tender wall shrubs in winter with a duvet of straw sandwiched between wire netting.

- Provided the plants are not too old, an overgrown box hedge can be coaxed back into shape over two seasons. Cut back the top and one side the first year, then trim the remaining side the second year.

- Instead of applying shading or using blinds in the greenhouse, try a 'live' screen of *Rhodochiton atrosanguineus*. Not only does this keep out the sun, it also shows off the pendant wine-red flowers.

- Cut off and burn the leaves of *Helleborus orientalis* in autumn. Not only does this set off the flowers and make them more prominent, it also helps to control hellebore leaf spot, which causes dark patches on the foliage, stems and flowers.

- When you plant a new tree, bury a length of tubing, about 45cm (18in) long and 5cm (2in) in diameter, in the planting hole, leaving the end just proud of the soil surface. This allows you to apply water directly to the root area where it is needed.

- If cats are a persistent problem in your garden, deter them with holly leaves sprinkled over the offending ground.

- Cat owners who are keen to see more birds in their garden could attach a small bell to the collar of their pet to warn birds of their presence.

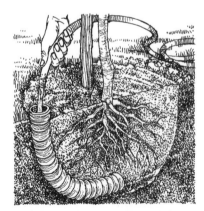

A root-watering system can channel the water directly to thirsty tree roots.

Holly leaves sprinkled on the ground help to deter cats.

Chapter 6

Peat Alternatives

Knightshayes Court, Devon

Since the 1950s peat has played a great part in the horticultural industry as a reliable growing medium because it is sterile, light-weight, pleasant to handle and has good water and air holding qualities. But over the last fifteen years or so, an argument has been raging between the peat producers and conservationists as to the long-term effects of peat extraction. Michael Hickson at Knight-shayes Court in Devon is involved in a series of trials looking for alternatives. A report is not expected until 2001 but in this chapter he suggests how to get good results from coir-based composts and growing media.

History of the garden

Area: 101 hectares (250 acres)
Soil: heavy, fertile, gravelly loam over clay base; acid–neutral
Altitude: 122–152m (400–500ft)
Average rainfall: 914mm (36in)
Average winter climate: moderate

One of the hallmarks of a good garden is its ability to satisfy on many levels. Knightshayes Court in Devon has such a garden because it appeals to a wide range of tastes, from complete novices, who are content to let the quiet beauty of the place lap over them, right through to experienced plantsmen and women, who flit butterfly-like from one rarity to another with all the excitement of children in a sweet shop. From the sheltered, sun-baked formal areas nearest the house to the more natural woodland glades beyond, it is not one garden but many.

The bones of an earlier Victorian layout, attributed to garden writer and designer Edward Kemp, still exist, but what visitors enjoy today is largely the joint creation of Sir John Heathcoat-Amory and his wife, Joyce, who reworked and softened the garden they inherited after their marriage in 1937. Their greatest legacy is undoubtedly the Garden in the Wood, an extensive area of exotic woodland, curving paths and glades which was annexed to the rest of the garden at a rate of about 0·8 hectares (2 acres) a year during the 1950s and 60s. Here shrub roses, rhododendrons, magnolias, pieris and acers, to name but a few, all vie for attention beneath the broken canopy of majestic pine, oak and beech trees, while shade-loving perennials such as pulmonarias, omphalodes, hellebores and geraniums stretch out at their feet.

Michael's background

Michael Hickson came to Knightshayes as Head Gardener in 1963, having spent seven years gaining a wide horticultural training. 'I feel it has become, in part, my garden because the Amorys brought me in as a team member,' he says. Such was his passion and commitment to the garden that they even named an area of woodland after him, where many of the best plant associations are to be found, including blue spruces with Japanese maples, and delicate ferns interwoven with hardy cyclamen. 'I just love growing plants and using them to their best advantage, whether it is for their structure, flowers, foliage, or just for the juxtaposition with other plants. At Knightshayes we run the National Trust's Plant Conservation Programme (PCP) and as a result we are sent seeds from all over the world and come into contact with other like-minded people. These are some of the best times of gardening. My life is connected with plants the whole time; I find them fascinating. For me the learning never stops.'

The peat debate

Peat forms when the soil is permanently waterlogged, and dead plants are in effect preserved rather than decomposed. There are three basic kinds of bog: blanket, fen and raised. It is this last type, which is created by a build-up of sphagnum moss in acidic water, that is of greatest interest to peat extractors because raised bogs can be many metres deep. But they are also greatly valued by conservationists because they provide rich habitats for many rare flowers, insects and birds, as well as preserve important archaeological remains.

In theory a living peat bog can regrow at about 15mm (½in) per year, but large-scale modern production has made this unlikely as land has to be drained prior to extraction. Not only is recolonisation by the native flora and fauna remote, but the complex water tables in adjacent undrained areas are also put under threat.

Peat and the National Trust

Although the National Trust gave up using peat for mulching and as a soil ameliorant in its gardens as long ago as 1991, its use was retained for propagation and potting composts because gardeners needed a reliable medium in which to grow and conserve the many rare and historically important plants under their jurisdiction. That said, a survey in 1992 found that 50 per cent of Trust gardens were not using any peat at all. However, following the Annual General Meeting in 1999, members voted overwhelmingly to phase out all use of peat in Trust gardens. As a result ADAS, independent land, horticultural and environmental consultants, were commissioned to undertake a year-long research programme to develop a range of peat-free and low peat potting composts. At time of writing, the first phase of trials have confirmed viable alternatives for the production of annuals, biennials and perennials are available; the Trust plans to go peat free in its own production of these lines in 2001. Further trials will be conducted in 2000 and 2001 to identify alternatives for trees, shrubs and ericaceous plants.

For a time the Trust used a natural waste product that comprises of recycled, rather than mined peat, which occurs as a by-product of the water industry in the Pennine area. Rainwater, charged with peat particles from the mountains and peat bogs, collects in reservoirs, and as part of the cleaning process, these particles must be removed by filtering.

Not only does the Trust want to eliminate peat in its own potting composts and to source alternative composts, it will be asking all commercial growers who supply plants to use an entirely peat-free medium. In this way it hopes to influence and encourage professionals and amateurs alike to try to find alternatives to this finite and ecologically sensitive resource.

It is only in exceptional circumstances where ericaceous plantings and raised peat beds are historically important that peat will still be allowed until a suitable substitute can be found. Such is the case at Knightshayes. Here, as an experiment, some of the peat block walls in the Garden in the Wood have been replaced with similar-sized blocks made up of pulverised rubber tyres. Now colonised by mosses and ferns, they blend in unobtrusively enough, but their main disadvantages are their high cost and the fact that they ooze white gum when new.

Using coir at Knightshayes as an alternative to peat

Knightshayes boasts an extensive nursery located near the former Victorian walled Kitchen Garden, which although not open to the public, supplies young plants for the garden's own use as well as raising some to be sold in the garden shop. The nursery also doubles as the site for the National Trust's Plant Conservation Programme, which accepts rare seed and young plants from around the world with a view to growing them on for distribution within the Trust, as well as propagating historically important species within its own organisation. Propagator Chris Trimmer says: 'It's like having three nurseries in one. Approximately 10,000 plants a year are raised from cuttings, as well as countless numbers from seed. I will also graft trees or shrubs where appropriate.'

All these plants are grown entirely in peat-free composts. 'We stopped using peat in the greenhouse sector ten years ago because it was thought that there should be an alternative. As a large propagation unit, I felt it was the right thing to do. Now it is proven to be so,' declares Michael. 'We have been using coir, but if the ADAS trials come up with something which turns out to be British then so much the better. Coir is a difficult issue, as I see it. I would rather use something that didn't have to be brought in from overseas, but if ships are going out to Sri Lanka loaded with goods and returning empty, it makes sense to come back with something and help the local economy into the bargain. That said, we are certainly going to look at other alternatives.'

Coir, which is derived from coconut husks, is bought in as compressed blocks, each one making about 100 litres of friable coir compost. A mattock is first used to break them into pieces, then they are soaked in water for about an hour before being finely shredded. 'It looks like peat, handles like peat and works just like peat,' says

Coir, as a compressed brick, will become friable compost when soaked in water.

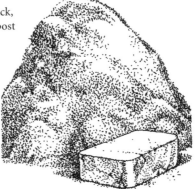

Chris. 'In fact for propagation, particularly cuttings, it is 100 per cent better than peat because it is more fibrous and open so creating a much better root system.'

The main difference with coir has been the approach to watering. 'It's a visual thing. You can see when peat is dry because it starts contracting away from the side of the pot. With coir the top layer dries out but the bottom remains moist, so it is much easier to kill a plant by overwatering,' explains Michael.

The main composts used at Knightshayes are given below:

- **General potting compost**

  6 parts coir

  3 parts sterilised loam (made up of 2 parts loam and
      1 part sterilised leafmould collected from the garden)

  2 parts 5–8mm washed quartz grit

  300g slow-release fertiliser per cubic metre of compost

- **General cuttings compost**

  Equal parts of coir and 4mm grit

- **Seed compost for trees, shrubs and herbaceous**

  3 parts coir

  2 parts sterilised loam

  1 part 3–4mm grit

- **General seed compost for annuals**

  These will be sown in pure coir compost as they are only in their trays for a few weeks before they are pricked out into the general potting mix above.

Early results of the ADAS trials indicate that it is possible to replace coir in the general potting compost with a combination of bark and a composted by-product of the forestry industry.

Soil conditioners

The soil at Knightshayes is best described as fertile Devon marl (clay), overlying a bedrock of stone. 'It is good soil, but very hungry. Any leaves that naturally sit on the beds are quickly taken down by worms,' says Michael. Indeed, decomposed leaf litter, or leafmould, makes an excellent soil conditioner, and in this garden with its large tracts of woodland there is no shortage of the raw material.

The borders are raked by hand to avoid too much soil loss, but the grass paths are blown clear with hand-held leaf blowers. Because of the size of the estate, a tractor-mounted leaf blower tackles the extensive sweeps of lawn. Attached to a large trailer an independent impellor draws in the leaves rather like a vacuum cleaner, cutting them up as it does so. They are then piled up into huge heaps and turned occasionally by tractor. As the leaves have already been chopped smaller before reaching the stack, they rot down very quickly and are ready for use within about twelve months, effectively halving the time that is usually recommended to make good leaf-mould. On a domestic scale, passing leaves through a shredder before composting them will have a similar effect.

Grafting as a method of propagation

As part of his work on the Plant Conservation Programme, Chris must be able to successfully propagate a very wide range of subjects, from the most diminutive alpines right through to the loftiest trees. The technique of grafting, which involves joining a shoot or bud from one plant (the scion) to the root system of another (the root-stock), plays a small but important role in his duties. Grafting as a means of propagation has several advantages over stem cuttings. The main one is that the ultimate size of the plant can be restricted depending on the rootstock. It is also a quick means of producing lots of plants from one bud-stick, as well as being a useful way of promoting earlier flowering.

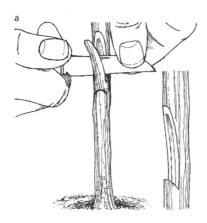

Propagating through grafting. A chip is removed from the rootstock (a). An identical chip is cut from the bud-stick (b) and placed into the stem of the rootstock (c). The bud chip is held firmly in position with clear tape (d). The rootstock is then cut back so that the grafted bud becomes the leader the following season (e).

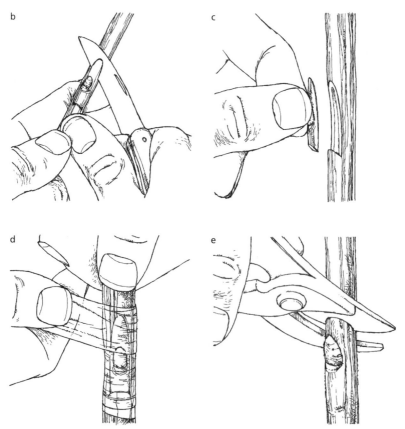

Recently Chris had to propagate an old perry pear cultivar found growing in a conifer woodland at Dyrham Park in Somerset, by a process known as budding. This works well on all rosaceous plants as well as magnolias. His methods are described below:

- Plant a suitable rootstock – such as the moderately vigorous Quince A or B for pears – in a pot or in the open ground. Only those of pencil thickness are suitable for budding.

- From mid- to late August select a bud-stick with plump, healthy buds from the current year's growth.

- About 15cm (6in) up from the base of the plant, make a 6mm (¼in) cut into the rootstock stem, at an angle of 45° (a). Make another incision about 2·5cm (1in) higher and slice down to meet the first cut. Remove the chip (b).

- Having first removed the leaf flush with the stem, make an exactly similar cut on the bud-stick, ensuring the bud is in the middle (c).

- Slip the bud-chip into position and tightly wrap the bud and stem with clear budding tape. Leave in position for about six weeks until the bud has united with the rootstock (d).

- In February or March cut back the rootstock, making an angled cut just above the bud, which will grow out to form the leader the following season (e).

Moss as a groundcover

In parts of the woodland, moss is positively encouraged beneath the canopy of trees, where it hugs the ground as an impenetrable green carpet but also creates its own contours, rising here, dipping there. 'In my opinion, moss is as beautiful as any lawn. There are so many different species and colours, from the darkest green to those that appear almost silver. To be honest, it's a world I know very little about but I love the way the dappled light catches it,' says Michael. The more acidic the soil, the better mosses like it. The ground is never cultivated so very few weed seeds are ever brought to the surface to germinate. The occasional dandelion seed, blown in by the wind, may settle sometimes, but is easily removed by hand.

Moss makes an attractive groundcover below trees at Knightshayes.

Tips

- If flying insects such as aphids and whitefly are a problem, spray them with insecticidal soap, which is based on the potassium salts of fatty acids and works by sticking their wings together. It will not kill their eggs, though, so you have to carry out a number of follow-up sprays, normally at seven day intervals, to be sure of eradicating them after they have hatched out. The best time to spray is in the evening to avoid sun scorch.

- When planting, don't just look at the plant from one angle. Look at it from all sides and consider how the sun will catch it throughout the day and throughout the seasons.

Chapter 7

Groundcovers, Lawns and Weeds

Cotehele, Cornwall

Winning the battle against weeds without chemicals is one of the toughest challenges that gardeners face. However, by remembering the old maxim that 'a weed is a plant growing in the wrong place' and learning to tolerate them in certain situations, you can immediately reduce the need for chemical warfare. At Cotehele in Cornwall, John Lanyon has a variety of strategies in place for managing the problem, which range from a broad acceptance of their presence in a wildflower meadow, to digging out whole borders to ensure that they are weed-free. Other useful techniques include mulching and using groundcover plants beneath trees and shrubs to suppress weeds and create additional year-round interest with the minimum of fuss.

History of the garden

Area: 7.6 hectares (19 acres)
Soil: acid/loam
Altitude: 76m (250ft)
Average rainfall: 1,143mm (45in)
Average winter climate: mild

Nestled among woods high above the west bank of the River Tamar lies the biscuit-coloured granite and slatestone house of Cotehele. Arranged around a series of enclosed courtyards, the building, with its gables and battlements, looks in on itself, as if shutting out the rest of the world. Little altered since the fifteenth century when the first stones were laid, it seems to be enveloped in its own bubble of tranquillity. The approach to the garden along high-banked narrow lanes that dip and climb at every turn, is spangled with primroses, ferns and pennywort, and only serves to heighten its remoteness and timelessness.

For nearly six hundred years, until the estate passed to the National Trust in 1947, it was owned by the Edgcumbe family. Although the medieval stewpond and charming domed dovecote hint at an earlier age, the present layout of the garden largely dates back to Victorian times, when many new introductions were planted.

There is a mandatory Valley Garden (which of course no self-respecting Cornish property should be without), but Cotehele is far more complex and satisfying than that. As you make your way along, secret gardens are revealed and surprises unfold. Be sure to go the right way round for the full effect. Intimate courtyards open onto a wildflower meadow; a low gateway gives onto the Upper Garden with its sublime borders and waterlily pool; the cut flower and foliage gardens lie beyond, concealed by dark yew hedges. The top path that skirts along the top of the meadow brings you down through an acer grove before opening out in front of the house with its formal terraces and shrub roses. In stark contrast a cool, dark tunnel beneath the lane emerges at the head of the informal Valley Garden – the best surprise of all.

Planted to resemble a Himalayan glade, the trees and shrubs romp away thanks to the damp mild climate. The huge hemlocks dominating the valley, which were planted in 1963 and have already been thinned out, bear testament to this. Below them the interwoven canopy is made up of a wide variety of acid-loving plants that luxuriate in such protected surroundings: hamamelis, camellias, rhododendrons, magnolias, embothriums, cornus and eucryphias, to name but a few. Cotehele also has its fair share of rarities: the umbrella pine (*Sciadopitys verticillata*) and Chinese yellow wood (*Cladrastis sinensis*) flourish here.

John's background

John Lanyon, along with his two members of staff, is the man responsible for this 7·6-hectare (19-acre) garden. Even as a child he knew he wanted to garden. After studying horticulture at the Royal Horticultural Society's garden at Wisley, then at Cannington College in Somerset and finally at the Royal Botanic Gardens, Kew, he joined the Trust on a short term contract, whereby he gained valuable experience in three high-profile Cornish gardens: Trelissick, Trengwainton and Glendurgan. After a three-year interlude at Rosemoor Gardens in Devon, John was once more lured back to the Trust as Head Gardener of Cotehele in 1998. He brings youth, energy and enthusiasm to the job.

John is an instinctive gardener: whatever he does comes from the heart as well as the head. 'Gardens are always more successful if you manage them sympathetically,' he says. 'That means working with the conditions, rather than fighting them, and using appropriate plants. If you constantly have to resort to chemicals, you are doing something wrong, and fighting nature rarely results in success.' Not only is he acutely aware of the needs of his plants, he is also sensitive to the garden's atmosphere. 'One of the great things about Cotehele is that it has so many different areas, each with its own character. I am trying to develop the garden so that each one has its own spark, its own flavour.'

Learning to tolerate weeds

'A weed is only a plant growing in the wrong place,' as the saying goes. Viewing them as such can bring a level of tolerance that is truly liberating for a gardener. Take dandelions, for example, a brazen little plant with striking yellow flowers. Think of all the time and effort you can save yourself if you dig them from borders but leave them in less manicured areas such as wildflower meadows.

At Cotehele John is not a weed fascist. 'Many plants just seed around, and as long as they are in the right place we just leave them because it adds to the mood of the place. This is Cotehele and some areas should look a bit rough around the edges, a few self-sown 'weeds' can actually add definition. That's why we tend to leave plants like honesty and the blue-flowered alkanet (*Pentaglottis sempervirens*),' he says. Similarly, ivy-leaved toadflax (*Cymbalaria muralis*) has colonised the crevices within the walls and cobbles of the Retainers' Court, so pitted are they with age. But because they lend the scene an air of romance, John will not be too fussy when he weeds the area.

Weed control

In common with many Trust gardeners, John does not relish the idea of using chemicals in the garden at all, but considers herbicides a necessary evil in the struggle to eradicate perennial weeds when time and resources are in short supply. However, that is not to say he favours them over simple digging, which he often employs as his first line of defence. His methods of controlling weeds are outlined below. Not only do they depend on the type of weed but also on the situation in which it is growing:

- **Bindweed**

Attractive it may be with its white trumpet flowers, but bindweed is an unwelcome visitor that crops up all too frequently at Cotehele. It plagues most of the garden but is a particular menace in the borders of the Upper Garden. However John and his team scored a victory over this insidious creeper, with its thick spaghetti roots, by eradicating it totally from one of the beds. 'We took out all the plants we wanted to keep, leaving a core of shrubs that were too large to move, then we dug the area thoroughly, removing every piece of root,' he explains. The ground was left empty for a whole year, and any shoots that subsequently emerged were traced back and dug out or sprayed

Encouraging bindweed to grow up bamboo canes in the border makes it easier to treat with glyphosate herbicide.

with glyphosate (see p.30). The base of the hedge, in all probability the source of the problem in the first place, was also cut back and the bindweed carefully treated.

'Just spraying with glyphosate only seems to turn the shoot blind, it does not kill the whole root system of the plant. Total eradication is much more successful if you are prepared to dig up the bulk of the roots first, or at least to chop them up to make them smaller. The spray is then much more effective,' thinks John.

Of course it is vital to put back clean plants. His triumph was nearly short-lived, much to his staff's amusement, when he introduced a plant from his own garden that turned out to have bindweed snaking through its roots. Once noted, it was swiftly dug out, cleaned and replanted. The border has so far remained a perennial weed-free zone.

Although present, bindweed is less of a problem in the more natural environment of the Valley Garden. 'There is no way we could dig it out because of all the existing trees and shrubs so we tend to pull off the top growth to weaken it. If it does get out of control, we push in bamboo canes nearby. The bindweed then grows up the canes making it easier for us to treat with glyphosate,' he says.

• Brambles

Although a haven for wildlife, brambles are a real scourge in the

Valley Garden because they come in from the surrounding woodland, swallowing up great tracts of border as they go. They spread rapidly by producing roots at the tips of their long thorny stems and by seeds spread by birds and other animals. If a large area is to be cleared, John sprays them with brushwood killer, which is effective on woody plants, then digs and pulls out what is left. Where sprays cannot be used, for example if brambles are growing among prized trees and shrubs, they will be dug out. 'We have found that strimming helps to stop brambles tip layering,' John explains.

- **Annual weeds**

Cotehele has the usual complement of annual weeds such as groundsel, speedwell, shepherd's purse and sow-thistles but they rarely become a problem. 'The best way to keep down annual weeds is to manage the borders properly. If they are planted appropriately and growing well, they look after themselves for much of the time. Occasionally we get problems at the back of borders when plants lean forward. The gap allows in light, causing weed seeds to germinate,' says John.

Much of the weeding in the Upper Garden is done by hand to avoid precious seedlings like eryngiums, meconopsis and *Knautia macedonica* being chopped off by over-zealous hoeing. This also means that the soil surface is continually worked. As John says, 'Forking is really important. Not only does it get rid of weeds, it also aerates the soil. People don't do it enough.'

In the Cut Flower Garden, where plants such as chrysanthemums, agapanthus, helichrysum, dahlias and statice are all grown in neat rows, hoeing is *de rigueur*. This is carried out when the weather is dry and sunny so weeds wilt, but while there is still moisture just below the soil surface. 'It is best to hoe regularly when the weeds are small,' says John. 'The aim is to cut them off at the neck, about 1mm below the surface, so they do not regrow. I use a big Dutch hoe, but we also have an American hoe with a pivoting blade.'

Paths

'Keeping the paths free of weeds is one of the biggest headaches at Cotehele,' John admits. 'And it matters. It really shows if they are scruffy.' Unfortunately this entails spraying with herbicides, albeit a small amount. 'In the Valley Garden I'm trying to manage the paths so they don't need so much work. The steep slope together with the high rainfall means they wash out easily, but if we can settle down the surface, the moss should grow and hold them together. They would look more natural too. Getting the surrounding planting right will also help. At the moment there is too much grass and this creates grass seedlings all over the paths. Planting something more appropriate would significantly reduce the potential weed problem.'

Groundcovers

Using groundcover plants to cover bare patches of soil is one of the most important ways to reduce weeds in the garden, and it is one that John exploits to the full at Cotehele. 'I am really conscious that we haven't got time to hand weed the Valley so we are now under-planting the trees and shrubs with plants that give more interest throughout the year.' Sharing pole position in the list of possible contenders are ferns and symphytum, both of which suit the conditions and give the right feel to the Valley Garden. 'Whatever we use has to be big, butch, bomb-proof, strimmer-proof and generally able to put up with abuse, otherwise you can forget it!' he laughs. By this means John hopes to do away with all the grass, nibbling away at it bit by bit; in its place will be a mosaic of colour and leaf texture. Not only will this reduce the time spent weeding, it will also dispense with the need to mow on difficult slopes.

Some of the most effective groundcover plants at Cotehele that are suitable for most soil types are listed below, together with John's comments about them:

Phuopsis stylosa

Ajuga reptans **'Catlin's Giant'** Creeping evergreen perennial with bronze-purple foliage and dark blue flowers. 'This needs to be planted in moist soil in partial shade to do well.'

Aubrieta × *cultorum* Mound-forming evergreen perennials with small single or double flowers in shades of white, pink and purple. 'They are excellent under roses, but you must cut them back after flowering to keep them tidy.'

Epimedium **(barrenwort)** Low, spreading perennials with heart-shaped leaves and spring flowers. The foliage of deciduous species is best cut down in late winter to show off the flowers to their best advantage. '*E. perralderianum* is one of the best evergreen cultivars with its bright yellow flowers; *E.* × *rubrum* is my favourite deciduous one with its red and yellow blooms. We cut it down in winter because the new leaves are a stunning red.'

Hardy geraniums (cranesbill) Long-lived undemanding perennials for a variety of situations:
G. × *cantabrigiense* 'Biokovo' is compact but has long runners. 'It is a cracking little plant with glossy foliage and whitish-pink flowers, and is good for smaller areas.'
G. macrorrhizum has sticky, strongly aromatic foliage that colours well in the autumn, and pinkish-purple flowers. 'It is good for large areas in shade.'

Comfrey, *Symphytum*

G. procurrens is a spreading plant with dark purple-pink petals, each with a black mark at its base. 'It's a bit of a thug but it is great in the dry soil among shrubs in the Valley.'

Phuopsis stylosa Mat-forming perennial with pink puffball flowers during summer. 'This works well in the rose beds.'

Salvia forsskaolii Clump-forming perennial with large, bristly leaves, producing white and blue flowers from June to early autumn. 'Does best in dappled shade.'

Saponaria ocymoides Ground-hugging perennial with a profusion of bright pink flowers in summer. 'It looks like a dwarf campion and is very good with roses.'

***Symphytum* (comfrey)** A robust perennial with rough, heart-shaped leaves and small tubular flowers, beloved by bees. *S. ibericum* (syn. *S. grandiflorum*) has pale yellow flowers; 'Hidcote Blue' and 'Hidcote Pink' are equally attractive, with flowers that fade with age. 'It is very easy to increase, you just pull a bit off and dab it in the ground. It smothers everything and looks fantastic on the banks when it flowers.'

Tolmiea menziesii Small perennial with the curious habit of producing young plants on the backs of older leaves. 'Good in partial or deep shade.'

Vinca (**periwinkle**) Low-growing, glossy-leaved evergreen with star-like flowers in early spring. *V. difformis* has pale blue, nearly white flowers; *V. major* 'Variegata' has creamy-white variegated foliage and blue flowers; *V. minor* 'Alba Variegata' has white flowers and yellow variegated leaves; *V. minor* 'Atropurpurea' has purple flowers; and *V. minor* 'Gertrude Jekyll' is compact with profuse white flowers. 'All are really good.'

Mulches

A mulch is a material that is used to cover the surface of the soil to suppress weed growth, to retain moisture and to maintain a cool root run. Mulches of organic origin such as well-rotted manure, garden compost, bark and straw will eventually rot down and help to improve the structure of the soil and also add valuable nutrients. Non-biodegradable mulches also have their uses. For example, black polythene will clear an area of perennial weeds, if left in place long enough, and gravel makes an attractive, hard-wearing surface.

The soil at Cotehele is best described as a slightly acid, open loam, which tends to dry out quickly, with the exception of parts of the Valley Garden that hold the moisture. 'We always plant accordingly and we look after the soil by mulching and forking it over. This is a very important method for keeping the borders clean. Growth starts early here, and because we are trying to retain the moisture in the top borders, we will mulch in mid-winter after the beds have been cut back. If we delay until spring the plants have made so much growth that the rain just hits the foliage and evaporates, leaving the soil below dry,' John explains. The following are his favoured mulches at Cotehele, together with his comments about them:

• mushroom compost in the borders of the Upper Garden. 'It's light, clean, easy to use and fairly cheap. Worms will take some of it down into the soil, helping to improve its structure.' See also p.118.

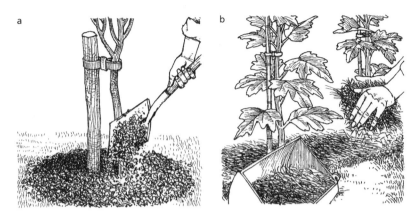

Biodegradable mulches: (a) bark chippings around the base of a newly planted tree; (b) Grass clippings around chrysanthemums.

- well-rotted manure in the Cut Flower Garden. Run along similar lines to a vegetable plot, this is a productive garden with flowers being grown as crops and replaced annually. To maintain soil fertility John applies manure, which is particularly rich in nitrogen.

- leafmould in the Valley Garden. 'As the garden is open all year round we clear the leaves every week. They are blown off the paths straight onto the surrounding planted areas, where they slowly rot down. They are a useful resource and help to enrich the habitat.'

- bark chippings in the Valley Garden. 'If we need to remove trees or shrubs we try to chip on site and put it back on the soil as a mulch (a). It also saves having to cart it away. I also use it around the base of newly planted trees to reduce weed competition.'

- grass cuttings around the plants lined out in the nursery beds (b). 'The secret is not to overdo it: about 5cm (2in) is enough otherwise it goes too slimy. It is also useful around the chrysanthemums in the Cut Flower Garden.'

- black woven plastic, such as Mypex, beneath the pots on the nursery. 'This greatly reduces weed seedlings germinating in the pots.

The beauty of it is you can lift it up and shake it off like a tablecloth. We also use it to cover the compost bins to keep out weeds.'

Lawns

How an area of grass looks depends very much on how it is used and how often it is mown. 'The lawns needn't look immaculate here because they wouldn't suit the place. The three areas where they must be smarter are the Bowling Green, the Terraces and the Upper Garden. Everywhere else we let daisies and other wild flowers grow because it is Cotehele and it doesn't really matter,' says John.

- **For a neat sward**

When the grass starts into growth, usually the beginning of March, lawn sand, which contains nitrogen and iron in the form of ferrous sulphate, is applied to kill moss and give growth a fillip from its winter slumbers. If time allows the treated areas will be scarified (raked vigorously) to remove the thatch, and then mown to tidy them up. Thereafter John and his team will mow every week. 'There is a horrendous amount of grass cutting at Cotehele because it just keeps growing. As we are continually removing growth to make them look smart, the lawns become starved and turn yellow unless we feed them. So we apply another feed from mid- to late April. I would like to try seaweed-based products or pelleted chicken manure in future, as both are said to work well.'

The main scarification is carried out in autumn before the grass stops growing to allow it to recover. John is keen to experiment by top-dressing the lawns with mushroom compost, which he hopes will improve their health. Bare patches are also renovated at this time using fine grass seed as these tend to be the most drought-tolerant species.

- **For meadow areas**

  Spangled with a myriad of old-fashioned, papery narcissus, whose parentage is now untraceable and long forgotten, the meadow is at its peak around Easter. The grass is left uncut until the beginning of July, leaving time for the bulbs to build up their reserves for the following spring. To prevent any real enrichment of the soil, which would encourage the growth of coarse grasses, the clippings are taken away and composted or used directly as a mulch around trees. 'It is topped off once or twice to keep it tidy. And besides, all the wild flowers start to come back – not your classic wild flowers, but those more often thought of as weeds,' says John. For example, the dandelion-like hawkbit (*Leontodon sp.*) creates pools of golden yellow later on in the summer. To extend the season still further he is adding drifts of galtonias, camassias, fritillaries and cyclamen.

Tips

- Do not keep plants in their pots in the greenhouse any longer than you have to. Plant them outside and you do not need to water and feed them so frequently; they will also be less vulnerable to pests such as whitefly and vine weevil in the open ground.

- Nip out the ends of plants growing both in the greenhouse and outside. The shoot then becomes quite woody and is much less susceptible to aphid attack.

- Remove some panes of glass from the greenhouse during summer to keep temperatures down. This changes the atmosphere at night as it lets in dew. In addition you can spray the plants lightly with water in the evening to help them stay humid all night, which most greenhouse pests hate.

- Pinch out the tips of cuttings once their roots have filled the pots. Then you have healthy bushy specimens to plant out.

- Feed your soil with bonemeal, a slow-release organic fertiliser, to kick-start the activity of soil dwelling micro-organisms. 'I use it on everything, from planting trees and shrubs to sprinkling over the borders. I even mix it into potting composts. It's exceptional for improving the health of the soil, which in turn leads to healthy plants,' explains John.

- Leave some apples on the tree to encourage blackbirds and thrushes to your garden. They will also consume large numbers of slugs and snails.

- When selecting groundcover plants do not forget about ferns. 'They make brilliant groundcovers in the right places, particularly in a woodland setting. I think they are underrated just because they are expensive. You can usually split and divide them but people tend not to do that with ferns.' John recommends *Dryopteris erythrosora*, which has copper-red young foliage; *D. affinis* 'Cristata' (syn. 'Cristata The King'), arranged like a shuttlecock with arching fronds; and the native lady fern, *Athyrium filix-femina*.

Dividing a mature fern.

Chapter 8

Gardening with Wildlife

Rowallane, County Down

It should come as no surprise that recycling has an essential part to play in organic gardening. At Rowallane in County Down, Mike Snowden's sympathetic management of the varied habitats may attract all kinds of wildlife, but it also generates huge amounts of garden waste. However, Mike has abundantly proved that no garden clipping or scrap of paper need ever be wasted, by dreaming up ever more inventive uses for them, from lining hanging baskets with shredded office waste to developing a bracken-based compost that out-performs peat.

History of the garden

Area: 21 hectares (52 acres)
Soil: acid/loam
Altitude: 61m (200ft)
Average rainfall: 914mm (36in)
Average winter climate: mild

There are few other gardens that can boast such a string of eponymously named plants: *Viburnum plicatum* 'Rowallane'; *Hypericum* 'Rowallane'; *Chaenomeles × superba* 'Rowallane'; *Primula* 'Rowallane Rose' and *Crocosmia masoniorum* 'Rowallane Orange', all of which make outstanding additions to the border. This roll-call of garden worthies also gives some indication of Rowallane's horticultural significance, for it is one of the twentieth century's foremost British gardens.

Situated about 11 miles south of Belfast in the rolling countryside of County Down, the property, which was then a farm, was bought by Rev. John Moore in 1860. He gradually enlarged the farmhouse, added the stable block, built the walled garden and created the Pleasure Grounds, but much of the planting that visitors enjoy today is down to the creative genius of his nephew, Hugh Armytage Moore, to whom he bequeathed the property in 1903.

Hugh Armytage Moore's greatest gift was to work with what he found, gradually absorbing the rock-strewn, undulating fields and moulding them into his garden, which now covers about 21 hectares (52 acres). Here large-leaved rhododendrons, deciduous azaleas, embothriums and nothofagus species sit as comfortably into the landscape as the native Scots pine, beech and oak trees that surround them. It is this happy balance between the wild and the exotic that is such a potent characteristic of Rowallane. For this reason important views of the surrounding countryside, with its gorse and eruptions of rock left by the Ice Age, are deliberately kept open, lest you forget where you are when you find yourself surrounded by a heady mix of flourishing exotics such as tree heathers, paulownia and eucalyptus.

Mike's background

With his long white beard, Mike Snowden bears more than a passing resemblance to the smiling, painted gnomes that line his office window. Head Gardener at Rowallane for nearly twenty years, he retires at the end of 2000 after an illustrious career with the Trust that has spanned over three decades. He first joined the organisation as a propagator at Bodnant in North Wales then went on to spearhead the extensive restoration project at Erddig as Head Gardener. His presence will undoubtedly be missed, not only because of his infectious enthusiasm for the place but also because he is such an excellent communicator. I vividly recall seeing him in a short film, made by the BBC, in which he was talking about the memorable handkerchief tree, *Davidia involucrata*, with its white tissue-like bracts, that is growing in the Hospital at Rowallane (a walled enclosure that was set aside for sick cattle in the days when the property was still a farm). I suspect he may miss the garden too; 'I have plenty to keep me busy,' he assures with just a hint of sadness.

Recycling at Rowallane

'I am a strong advocate of recycling and managing the garden using its own resources,' admits Mike. 'This is not necessarily driven by the need to do things organically or because I wanted to jump on any present-day band wagon, but simply because it makes sound economic sense to recycle what already exists in the place and manage the garden's waste. Here we have an extremely natural garden with our own native flora growing alongside introduced exotics. And because it has always been like that I have simply plucked out of history the way we manage it. Its creator, Armytage Moore, was interested in the plants; he wasn't after fine lawns and he didn't landscape. He used to cut the hay meadows twice a year with a horse-drawn reaper. We carry on that tradition, (albeit with a tractor-mounted cutter), which produces copious amounts of waste during the year's management. Not only are there the cuttings from the hay meadows, there are also the leaves, shreddings and prunings from the rest of the garden. They all go together to produce compost, which we then return as mulches, rather than burning them all and buying in organic material.'

About 150–200 tons of compost are generated every year, so its cumulative effect is not to be scoffed at, especially on Rowallane's thin neutral to acid soil. In the area affectionately known by the garden staff as 'the Dump', a series of exemplary compost heaps mature away nicely. Flat-topped and straight-sided, they are colossal, even by the Trust's standards. Measuring about 7m long by 4m wide by 4m high (22ft × 12ft × 12ft), they are built up by hand but turned later with a tractor fitted with a front loader. Despite their size, the principles of layering the waste throughout the heap still apply. For every 30cm (12in) of loose material, a topping of manure follows. 'This contains much of the micro-life which will kick-start the compost,' Mike explains. Grass clippings, garden waste, including annual weeds and spent flower stems, are all utilised. Woody prunings are passed through a shredder first to speed up the decomposition process (see also pp.24 and 46). Each heap takes about two years to rot down, but the end result, by Mike's own admission, is 'superb.'

In true recycling spirit, nothing is ever wasted. Mike even persuaded the administrative staff at the Trust's regional office at Rowallane to shred their unwanted paper and second-hand memos. Not only is this incorporated as layers into the compost heaps, it is also used to fill wire baskets which are placed in the leat that feeds the large pond in the Pleasure Ground. These baskets serve to catch any slurry and run-off from the surrounding fields before it reaches the pond, so helping to keep the water clear and algae-free. This dirty filter paper, which is periodically replaced, also ends up on the compost heaps.

Bracken as a peat alternative

For the last fifteen years the gardeners at Rowallane have been making their own peat-free potting composts, substituting their own composted bracken in place of peat to make a general John Innes type mix. 'We use an old recipe I picked up donkey's years ago in Yorkshire. Traditionally the foresters would construct seedbeds or 'lazy beds' in which to sow their tree seeds. There was a saying, which was on the lines of this: 'If the lazy bed were made from composted barley straw, there was copper beneath it; if it were made from composted wheat straw, there was silver beneath it; and if it were made from composted bracken, there was gold beneath it.' I reckoned bracken must be pretty good so we gave it a try. Also I'm mean. I didn't want to pay good money for peat if there was something we could get for nothing!' laughs Mike.

The resulting compost proved to be outstanding and is used for potting up and potting on as well as for seed sowing, although admittedly it must be rubbed through a sieve to make it fine enough for the latter. Bracken is cut back just after it has started to turn colour in autumn and is composted separately. After a year it is ready for use. Unlike peat, which has few nutrients, bracken is rich in phosphates and has a good spongy structure, which holds up well in a pot. 'We have to cut down the bracken anyway, but this way we are producing a useful product into the bargain,' says Mike.

The potting mixes used at Rowallane are outlined below (see also pp.50 and 88).

- The first follows a John Innes type formula and is ideal when loam is available:

7 parts sterile loam
3 parts composted bracken
2 parts coarse sand

- The second substitutes well-rotted garden compost when loam is unavailable:

5 parts well-rotted garden compost
2 parts composted bracken
2 parts coarse sand

Attracting wildlife and managing pests

Although passionately interested in wildlife and the natural world, Mike does not pretend to garden without the use of herbicides. 'We do use minimal amounts of glyphosate (see p.30) applied with a controlled droplet applicator simply because it saves on labour. I always say it is not the use, but the misuse of chemicals that causes problems, and the more you can cut back the better.'

That said, very few other sprays are used; Mike prefers to let nature take care of the pests where possible. 'The key is to have a situation whereby you are not breaking any wildlife cycles; if you interfere and pluck out one element, you risk ruining the whole thing. For example, we do get rabbits in the garden but we also have foxes and stoats that come in from the surrounding countryside, thereby establishing a balance which we can cope with, quite honestly.' Similarly, at Rowallane, slugs and snails are not the scourge most people consider them to be because there is a burgeoning frog population. 'Although I use a few on the nursery, I never have to put down slug pellets in the garden, there's just no need. I count us very lucky because the frogs are just part and parcel of the life cycle here. I still get as much fun out of seeing frogspawn now as I did when I was three,' he laughs.

Because of the varied habitats that exist at Rowallane (see below) the range of birds that inhabit the garden is truly impressive. Mike keeps a comprehensive list of those spotted each month, in the hope that one day it will form part of the information available to visitors in the interpretation centre about what he terms 'our other visitors'. Tree creepers, gold crests, ravens and moorhens are just a few of the bird species that are found here, but it is also well known as a haunt for bats, including pipistrelles, Daubenton's and long-eared bats.

As well as refraining from using chemicals, the best way to encourage wildlife and natural predators to the garden is to recreate the habitats found in nature. Many exist already at Rowallane; Mike merely exploits them through sympathetic management.

- **Hay meadows**

'The grassland here has never been improved. It consists of old farm pasture land that is very pure, very species-rich,' explains Mike. Native wild orchids, including early purples, *Dactylorhiza fuchsii*, twayblades and butterfly orchids, flourish on the upper slopes in the Pleasure Ground and in the Hospital.

How often the grass is cut and at what height varies according to the area of the garden and what is growing in it. For example, in the

Spring Ground the grass is spangled with naturalised daffodils and lady's smock, *Cardamine pratensis*. It is mown when the bulbs' foliage has died down, usually around mid- to late June, which co-incides with the traditional time to make hay. Thereafter it is rotary mown just once, to make it look as though it has been grazed, then it is left to grow. Come July the whole of the hillside is awash with blue from devil's bit scabious, *Succisa pratensis*. To increase the scabious still further, Mike thrashes the stems with a stick to dislodge the ripe seed before the area is once more cut in late August. At the bottom of the slope, where the soil is much richer and the grass much coarser, the sward is maintained at grazing length, about 8–10cm (3–4in), to encourage buttercups and daisies. In the orchid areas the grass is left until August, while the rest is cut at grazing height to encourage lots of variation.

'The hay meadows are wildlife-friendly because we haven't broken any of the life cycles of the insects, mammals and birds,' explains Mike. In fact, his management has been so successful that the long-eared owl population in the Pleasure Ground has continued to rise steadily over the years. This is due to the maintenance of their food supply – namely mice and voles – that live in the long grass.

• Pond

The large pond in the Pleasure Ground forms part of a natural drainage course. Any form of water attracts wildlife, and this is no exception. Mallards, moorhens, eels, frogs, dragonflies and dam-selflies abound. It is also a breeding ground for midges, which are an important food source for bats, swifts and swallows. Mike has recently raised hundreds of *Fritillaria meleagris* bulbils, which have been planted in the damp ground adjacent to the pond. He feels a fritillary meadow is a fitting legacy to leave behind when he retires.

• Woodland edge habitat

The shelter belts around the garden play a significant part in its success, not just because they provide protection from the wind, but also because they create an important habitat for wildlife. The dominant trees are mostly beech, Scots pines and oaks. On the outer side where they meet the surrounding countryside, they are underplanted with a canopy of smaller subjects like field maple, holly, blackthorn and hazel to recreate a typical field fringe hedge. On the garden side rhododendrons, Portuguese laurel and holly play the leading role. What is particularly gratifying is the fact that red squirrels have returned to the garden after a very long absence. 'We think it is because the Scots pines are now maturing and beginning to produce cones so there is a ready food supply for them,' explains Mike.

- **Borders**

The greater the range of plants that is grown in the garden, the more wildlife will be attracted to it. Native subjects generally support the widest range of creatures because they have evolved side by side, but many introduced and exotic species can be just as valuable for their pollen and nectar-producing flowers or succulent autumn berries, as is so clearly demonstrated at Rowallane. Plants that flower very early in the season, such as hellebores, as well as those at the tail end, like asters, are especially worthy of a place in the border as they extend the natural food supply over as long a period as possible.

Mike delays cutting down the herbaceous plants until late February. 'Lots of beneficial insects such as ladybirds overwinter on

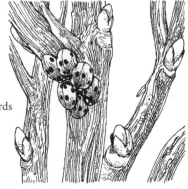

Overwintering ladybirds clustered on a twig.

Enkianthus campanulatus   *Eucryphia × nymansensis* 'Nymansay'

the dead stems. Also there's nothing to be gained from cutting them down any earlier because many still look really good throughout the winter. For example, *Clematis recta* has lovely swirling yellow stems, and the colour of *Sedum spectabile* seems to improve with age.'

Some of the best wildlife plants at Rowallane are outlined below, together with Mike's comments about them (see also pp.19-20, 58 and 128-9):

Bupleurum fruticosum Open, spreading evergreen shrub, growing to about 2m (6ft), with blue-green foliage and yellow cow parsley-like flowers from mid-summer to early autumn. Suitable for all soil types. 'It's incredible – the flowers are constantly alive with flies.'

Enkianthus campanulatus Large spreading tree-like shrub, growing to 5m (15ft) tall, with red-veined, creamy-yellow, bell-shaped flowers in early summer and stunning orange-red autumn colour. Requires an acid soil. 'It's a terrific insect plant.'

***Eucryphia* × *nymansensis* 'Nymansay'** Slightly tender, column-shaped, evergreen tree, growing to 15m (50ft), with attractive serrated foliage and cup-shaped white flowers in late summer. Does best on neutral to acid soil. 'This is invaluable for wildlife later in the year.'

Davidia involucrata (**handkerchief, or ghost tree**) Deciduous specimen tree for all soils, growing to 15m (50ft), producing small round flowerheads surrounded by papery white bracts in May. 'It's a good bat plant because of the night flying insects that visit it.'

Mahonia Evergreen shrubs for all soil types with handsome architectural foliage and fragrant yellow flowers in winter. 'They are a useful source of nectar when little else is in flower.'

Hoheria Genus of tender deciduous and evergreen trees and shrubs from New Zealand, grown mainly for their fragrant white flowers from mid- to late summer. Suitable for all soils. 'They are a good source of nectar for later in the season.'

Malus sargentii Spreading shrub or tree suitable for all soils. Grows to approximately 4m (12ft) tall by about 5m (15ft) wide, with masses of white scented blossom followed by tiny, long-lasting dark red apples. 'This is such a good plant for wildlife that it deserves to be grown much more widely. It doesn't get scab or mildew, and it is a great favourite with redwings and fieldfares.'

Rhododendrons Huge genus of deciduous and evergreen trees and shrubs for acid soils with showy and often very fragrant flowers, mostly borne in late spring. 'We have a huge range here at Rowallane, particularly the species. They start flowering in February and go on till about August, with a crescendo of colour in mid-May. Their nectar-rich flowers and freely produced seed support much insect life as well as birds. The evergreen species are a great favourite with blackbirds, robins and other birds that spend the winter scratching around below them in the leaf litter and mulch.'

The importance of ivy for wildlife

As a former farm, the garden has a legacy of dry-stone walls, which were built as a way of containing livestock. Many of them now are

Cutting back an overgrown ivy on a dry-stone wall.

enveloped by a thick blanket of common ivy, *Hedera helix*, which revels in the climate of Northern Ireland. 'If it is managed, it adds to the garden. Obviously there are places where it is not allowed to grow, but ivy is an important nectar source for the holly blue butterfly, many birds nest in it and insects overwinter on it. But it has a bad reputation. Dry-stone walls are often locked together by ivy, and if you start pulling it about, you will literally pull the wall to pieces.'

Mike roughly follows a three-year rotation when cutting back ivy, pruning it on some walls while leaving it to grow and set seed on others. 'We simply manage it as we do any other plant. Sometimes we don't get round to it until four years, but it doesn't really matter. The main thing is to get to it before it becomes so top heavy that it would pull over the wall.' Using loppers all growth is cut back tight against the wall in late winter or early spring before the birds have started to nest. It also ensures the ivy greens up quickly. Ideally, it is then left to grow for a further three years before the process is repeated. Managing ivy this way causes as little disturbance to the wildlife as possible, but also ensures it never gets too big for its boots.

If you inherit a wall with overgrown ivy, Mike suggests tackling it over three years to minimise disturbance of the creatures that depend on it. In the first year, cut back hard about a third of the ivy in late winter; in the second year, cut back the next third; and in the third year, cut back the final third. This should bring it back to a controllable level.

Tips

- Primulas, as well as a variety of plants grown in containers, are especially susceptible to vine weevils, whose soil-dwelling, curved white grubs chomp their way through roots, eventually killing the plant. They were a constant problem in the primula beds at Rowallane until Mike applied their biological control, *Heterorhabditis megidis*. A microscopic parasitic nematode, it is only effective when soil or compost temperatures exceed 12°C (54°F), so is best applied in late summer or early autumn. 'This has made such enormous inroads into them, they are no longer the problem they once were.'

- Mushroom compost together with grit makes a valuable top-dressing for lawns. At Rowallane it is stored for two years prior to use in order to leach out its natural lime content, and prevent it having a deleterious effect on the ericaceous soil. See also p.102.

- Shredded paper makes a wonderful lining for hanging baskets; brown shredded paper is even better as it is less obvious. 'So simple yet it works!' Mike enthuses.

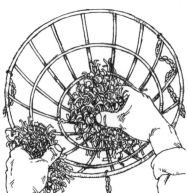

A hanging basket lined with recycled shredded paper.

Chapter 9

A Natural Garden

Glendurgan, Cornwall

Just as a good cook is never short of visitors, if you create a natural larder in your garden the chances are you will soon be blessed with creatures willing to eat it, helping to keep pests at bay in the process. At Glendurgan in Cornwall the wild flower meadows both support the local wildlife and look good all year round. In this chapter, Rob James explains how good management and a careful choice of plants can encourage animals and insects to set up home in your garden by ensuring that there is food available as they prepare for, and emerge from, hibernation.

History of the garden

Area: 10 hectares (25 acres)
Soil: acid/sandy loam
Altitude: 10–70m (33–230ft)
Average rainfall: 1,016mm (40in)
Average winter climate: mild

It is the interplay between open sweeps of meadow and the more intimate glades of trees and shrubs which sets apart Glendurgan from other Cornish valley gardens. Stand at the head of the ravine and look south, catching glimpses of the sparkling water of the Helford River far below, and this is most clearly demonstrated, particularly in late April and May, when the garden is at its most enchanting. A froth of spring blossom, provided mainly by flowering cherries, magnolias and *Viburnum plicatum* 'Mariesii', is punctuated here and there by vibrantly coloured rhododendrons; below them a shimmering sea of bluebells laps over the grassy banks to complete the picture.

The origin of Glendurgan stems back to the 1820s when the land was bought by Alfred Fox, a wealthy businessman from Falmouth who already rented cellars and orchards at Durgan, the tiny fishing hamlet from which the garden takes its name. To buffer the force of the wind, he set about establishing thick shelterbelts around the garden, consisting of native deciduous trees as well as recently introduced conifers from North America. These also provided the necessary protection for his extended and newly planted orchards. Although very little now remains, the memory of Alfred's passion for fruit trees still lives on. For example, the areas presently known as 'Lashbrook's Hill', 'Patterson's Orchard', 'Manderson's Hill' and 'Birch's Orchard', all take their names from the people who managed the apple orchards in his time.

As a keen gardener and practising Quaker, Alfred wanted to create a small piece of heaven on earth. Advantage was taken of the other Fox gardens, which supplied seeds and plants, but links within the family shipping agency were also exploited to bring into the country exotic and tender species from distant lands. Part of his Quaker belief was that space should be made for everything. That is why native wild flower glades were left to develop alongside the orchards and more exotic plantings.

As successive generations of the Fox family took over, and the cost of labour spiralled, so the orchard areas were reduced and the practice of introducing rare, tender and unusual trees and shrubs subsequently increased. Despite these changes, the wild flower meadows were not compromised; if anything they have become richer in species due to continued sympathetic management. In 1962 the Fox family donated Glendurgan to the National Trust, but they still live in the house and enjoy an involvement in the garden.

Rob's background

Rob James, although recently departed from the Trust for pastures new, has very fond memories of Glendurgan. He was taken on as

Head Gardener in 1990 partly as a response to the storms earlier in that year which devastated the garden. He was young, fit and had the ability to brandish a chainsaw with the comfortable ease that most of us wield secateurs. No mean feat when you consider the gradients of the garden! 'At the time I was a trainee at nearby Trelissick where I learnt an awful lot about woodland gardening skills. After the storms, Glendurgan needed someone with a knowledge of tree work and clearance as well as the horticultural element,' he explains. 'I particularly enjoyed the development work which meant, as a team, we could use our creative flair, but obviously within the confines of what the garden was about.'

He also admits that the mild climate acted as a magnet. 'It is always a challenge to garden on the edge of hardiness for the British Isles: you may suffer great failures but you also enjoy remarkable successes. The climate is a good leveller; it stops you getting carried away thinking you can grow everything when you suddenly get a cold winter and lose the tenderest subjects. It is part of the natural cycle of Cornish gardens, but it gives you the chance to make changes and allows the garden to move on.'

The wild flower meadows

The grassy banks studded with wild flowers create an ideal backdrop for the tender and exotic trees and shrubs, such as *Lomatia ferruginea*, *Michelia doltsopa*, *Musa basjoo* and *Cunninghamia konishii*, that rise above them. Beautiful in their own right, the meadows also allow warmth and light into the garden, and create a valuable habitat for wildlife such as butterflies, birds and small animals that rely on flowers and grasses as a source of food.

When the Trust took over the garden, one of its policies was to increase the native flora through sensitive management; another was to enhance what already existed by introducing carefully selected species that could naturalise themselves and look appropriate in

Ragged robin, *Lychnis flos-cuculi*

the setting. Even the most fastidious would be hard-pressed not to congratulate the Trust on its success on this score. First to throw off their winter wraps and sparkle in the early spring sunshine are primroses, violets, *Narcissus cyclamineus* and *N. pseudonarcissus.* Then come the bluebells, from the distance appearing at first as a watery blue wash over the grass, but later deepening in intensity until nearly all trace of green is masked. Next great swathes of aquilegias burst forth with tall, wiry stems and nodding heads of flowers in every shade from white through to red and blue. Ragged robin, or *Lychnis flos-cuculi*, with its spidery pink petals, and the scented yellow flowers of *Primula prolifera*, arranged in tiers up its slender stem, proliferate with gay abandon in the damper sites. As summer advances the valley regains its green patchwork mantle, peppered here and there with the native foxglove.

In addition, four species of orchid occur naturally on the banks at Glendurgan and their numbers are increasing steadily, which Rob finds particularly gratifying. Revelling along the woodland fringe is the early purple orchid which sends up its reddish-purple flower spikes from April to May, and the common twayblade, whose insignificant greenish flowers are easily overlooked. In sunnier, damper spots the pinkish-red marsh orchid blooms from June to July. But the real success story concerns the heath spotted orchid. 'In previous years there was just one but last year we had nine, which

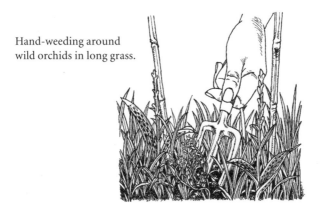

Hand-weeding around
wild orchids in long grass.

was wonderful, particularly as it produced pink as well as white flowers.' Their management involves painstakingly marking them with canes and hand-weeding round them, prior to strimming the areas in which they are growing. This results in their being able to increase naturally since their seeds ripen later than most other wild flowers.

Management of the wild flower meadows

To maintain and improve the diversity of flora in the meadows at Glendurgan a regime consisting of two cuts a year is adopted, as Rob explains:

- **The summer cut**

'This is carried out after the bluebells, aquilegias and candelabra primulas have set seed. Therefore we actually begin cutting by about mid-July and go through to the end of August. It takes about six weeks to do it all, starting near the house at the top and gradually working our way down to the bottom. On large areas we use a pedestrian operated machine with the blades set high – this allows slow-worms and other small animals to escape the chop; on steeper banks we use a strimmer. The cuttings are left to dry for between

Raking long grass vigorously to improve germination of wild flower seeds.

a week and a fortnight, and any seed that is left ripens and drops down into the remaining sward. We then rake off and compost the clippings to stop any real enrichment of the grassed areas. We discovered that raking the banks vigorously, a process similar to scarifying, actually improves the germination and spread of wild flowers because some of the thatch and moss is removed thus allowing seeds to get right down to the soil.'

- **The winter cut**

'The cycle is repeated, usually at the beginning of December when most of the deciduous trees have shed their leaves. This has the dual benefit of removing the fallen foliage and prevents spring bulbs and flowers being stifled before the growing season finally commences. It also gives them a head start as they do not have to fight their way through thick grass. Timing is crucial otherwise you would decapitate the bulbs that have started to come through already.'

Ideal plants for naturalising in meadows

Some plants are more suitable than others for naturalising in an existing grass sward or meadow. For example, highly bred cultivars with blowzy flowers look too bullish in a natural landscape, far more comfortable are the unadulterated species, from which these block-busters originally arose. The following are some of Rob's favourites, all of which will tolerate any soil type unless otherwise stated.

Galanthus nivalis (**common snowdrop**) A bulb with pendent white flowers from late winter. 'They are a lovely forerunner of spring, a real sign that winter is nearly over. At Glendurgan they start poking their heads through on sunny days just after Christmas. Moist, shady areas are their favoured sites, especially under the magnolias in the Cherry Orchard,' says Rob.

Narcissus cyclamineus An unusual daffodil with nodding, com-pletely reflexed petals. 'It is a dainty plant that seems happy in sun or partial shade as long as it has moist soil. We have naturalised it through the bottom of both Cherry and Birch's Orchard.'

Narcissus cyclamineus

Fritillaria meleagris (**snake's head fritillary**) A bulb with nodding, bell-shaped white or purple flowers with chequered markings. 'Although rare in the wild, it has not in fact been difficult to establish at Glendurgan in the moister areas of grass, despite our naturally acid soil.'

Primula veris (**cowslip**) A rosette-forming perennial with long stems and a topknot of scented yellow flowers. 'I love it but we can't grow it here because it prefers alkaline soils,' explains Rob.

Lychnis flos-cuculi (**ragged robin**) A perennial, growing to 75cm (30in), with star-shaped, deeply cut pink blooms. 'It is useful for us because it flowers into early summer, thereby extending our season. It must have moist soil, but does not mind sun or shade.'

Digitalis purpurea (**common foxglove**) A biennial with tall spikes of pink or purple tubular flowers. 'They may be boring but they provide such an effect and are great for wildlife. As they start flowering in June, once again, they extend our season.'

Echium vulgare (**viper's bugloss**) A bristly biennial with blue flowers. 'There is a constant buzz around this plant when it is in flower because the bees love it. We grow it in borders where plants have less competition from grasses, but once established, I think it would be robust enough to naturalise in meadow areas too.'

Hyacinthoides non-scripta (**English bluebell**) A bulb with nodding, scented blue blooms. 'The wild flower content at Glendurgan is at its best when the bluebells are flowering. They thrive throughout the garden but grow best in a bit of shade.'

Aquilegia vulgaris (**granny's bonnet**) A perennial with attractive, lobed foliage and nodding, spurred flowers. 'We have a complete range of colours here, from silvery-white right through to deep purply-black. They seed themselves around freely, and you never know what's going to come up. *En masse* they look stunning and visitors love them.'

Hermodactylus tuberosus (**widow iris**) A tuberous perennial with unusual greenish-yellow and velvety black flowers. 'This does well on the higher banks where it is drier, but also seems to tolerate a bit of shade. It never fails to take visitors by surprise when it is in flower.'

Conopodium majus (**pignut**) A perennial with a knobbly tuberous root, wonderful, fretted foliage and white flower umbels similar to cow parsley. 'Like most of the Umbelliferae, it is very attractive to insects.'

Creating a new meadow

Although Rob has never had to sow an entire meadow from scratch at Glendurgan, he has had to re-establish existing swards, for example where large trees were removed or where areas were altered. 'We found it difficult to introduce wild flowers and grasses and get the balance right. The best way was simply to be patient and let the existing plants colonise the area. As pioneer species, foxgloves and campions would establish themselves first, then after a few seasons the native grasses would come in, eventually it would end up looking very natural.'

Having said that, Rob gives the following tips if you want to create a new meadow:

- The best time to sow a wild flower meadow is during early autumn, as some species need a period of cold weather to break dormancy and germinate.

- Low fertility is the key to success, so if your chosen site is too rich, remove the top 5–7.5cm (2–3in) of soil for use elsewhere. The subsoil below will be poorer and better for the establishment of wild flowers.

- Ensure that any deep-rooted weeds are removed, either by thorough digging or spraying them with glyphosate to kill their roots.

Removing the topsoil to create a new meadow.

Cutting a young meadow
with a rotary mower.

- Prepare a fine crumbly seed bed by raking and firming the exposed surface, then sow the seed thinly and lightly rake it in.

- Choose flowers and grasses to suit your soil type, and bear in mind the situation – is it shady, exposed, damp or dry?

- An autumn-sown meadow should be cut at the beginning of June, leaving at least 7·5cm (3in) of growth to ensure strong root bases. Do this two or three times in the first year even if a few flower spikes appear.

- In subsequent seasons you can follow the cutting regime carried out at Glendurgan, as outlined previously.

Trees and shrubs for wildlife

The greater the range of plants that grow in the garden, the more wildlife it will support, enticed by nectar, pollen, seeds and berries to this natural larder. The more wildlife a garden attracts, the better pests will be kept at bay (or at more acceptable levels from the gardener's standpoint). Therefore, no matter how you look at the equation, plants that offer wildlife a food source are of great benefit to the environmentally-friendly gardener. From the wildlife's point of view very early and late flowering subjects are most valuable because they provide much-needed nourishment for insects emerging from or going into hibernation. Below are some of the most notable plants for wildlife at Glendurgan, including Rob's comments about them (see also pp.19-20, 58 and 115-16):

Bupleurum fruticosum A rounded, dense evergreen shrub, growing to about 2m (6ft), with blue-green foliage and small star-shaped, cow parsley-like yellow flowers from midsummer to early autumn. It is ideal for coastal gardens. 'Bees and insects love it.'

Euphorbia mellifera (**honey spurge**) A large, rounded, tender evergreen shrub, growing to about 2m (6ft) or more. In late spring pinky-brown, honey-scented 'flowers' (more correctly cyathia) are produced, followed by knobbly rounded fruit from late summer.

Salvia elegans '**Scarlet Pineapple**' (**pineapple sage**) An herbaceous perennial or subshrub with soft foliage that smells strongly of pineapple when crushed, and bright red flowers. 'All the salvias are great because they take our season right through to early autumn. This particular cultivar attracts the hummingbird hawk moth.'

Cornus capitata (**Bentham's cornel**) A spreading evergreen tree growing to 12m (40ft). In summer white or yellowish bracts are produced. The deciduous *C. kousa* is more conical in habit and smaller, reaching just 7m (22ft), with creamy-white bracts and striking autumn colour. 'Both species are blessed with unusual strawberry-like red fruits which the birds adore'.

Buddleja davidii (**butterfly bush**) A fast-growing deciduous shrub with arching, slightly pointed flowerheads in shades of white and pink through to blue and dark purple. 'We have many different cultivars of *B. davidii* that flower from summer into autumn. They are great for screening or as filler plants, and we use them for height where we are waiting for other things to establish. Although showy, they always seem to look natural in our landscape. As the common name implies, they are especially good for butterflies.'

Tips

- Rob and his team collect seed from different colonies of wild flowers within the garden, mix it up then scatter it around to ensure the genepool remains healthy and invigorated.

- If vine weevils are a problem on candelabra primulas, try watering on their biological control as soon as soil temperatures exceed 12°C (54°F) around August. 'It made a big difference at Glendurgan, and because it is host-specific it does not harm the water courses unlike pesticides,' explains Rob.

- If you have the space and squirrels are a problem plant a sycamore or two. The troublemakers will be attracted to the tree like a magnet and will hopefully leave your more ornamental plantings alone.

- If you have a large woodland garden, especially one on an awkward site, as at Glendurgan, try chipping or shredding directly back on to the soil, rather than carting away the prunings. This will save much time and energy, and the material will act as a weed suppressing mulch.

Chapter 10

Gardening Under Cover

Belton House, Lincolnshire

The sheltered conditions of a conservatory or greenhouse give the gardener the freedom to experiment with all manner of plants that are too tender for the rigours of the outdoors. However, such perfect growing conditions are equally conducive to pests, which thrive because their natural predators are thin on the ground. The temptation to spray is enormous, but much to the delight of Fred Corrin, biological controls have proved far more effective in the Orangery at Belton House in Lincolnshire than chemical insecticides. Here Fred identifies the main offenders and their predators, and explains how to achieve an equilibrium in the greenhouse.

History of the garden

Area: 14 hectares (35 acres)
Soil: neutral/sandy loam
Altitude: 52m (170ft)
Average rainfall: 686mm (27in)
Average winter climate: cold

Beneath huge skies, Belton House stands serene and elegant above its rolling Lincolnshire landscape. To the onlooker, its style and symmetry present a truly beautiful spectacle, enhanced all the more by its uncanny ability to radiate a warm glow, thanks to the locally quarried, golden Ancaster stone with which the mansion is faced.

Built in the 1680s for Sir John Brownlow, the Restoration country house architecture makes a fine backdrop for the gardens that now surround it. Few traces survive of the original layout, which was inspired by the highly elaborate, formal French gardens that were so popular at the time. Like many such schemes, it fell prey to the tide of changing fashions and was more or less swept away in the mid-eighteenth century by the new landscape style which was transforming the face of the English countryside. However, in the early nineteenth century, the 1st Earl Brownlow commissioned Jeffry Wyatville to redesign the area formerly occupied by the kitchen garden. The formal sunken Italian Garden was thereby created, with the Orangery at one end of its central axis, the Lion Exedra at the other, and a circular pool with a fountain in the middle. The original elaborate box-edged parterres have since been simplified for ease of maintenance. A second formal area, known as the Dutch Garden, was created to the north of the house in 1879 to form part of the 3rd Earl's neo-Caroline 'restoration' of Belton.

Fred's background

Belton House and its grounds were given to the National Trust in 1984 by the 7th Lord Brownlow. Ten years later in 1994, Fred Corrin, previously in charge of the gardens at Packwood House in Warwickshire, was appointed Head Gardener. He and his three members of staff are responsible for maintaining and manicuring the immaculate 14 hectares (35 acres) at Belton. 'I find my job satisfying for a number of reasons: I enjoy the beautiful surroundings and working outdoors, and various features like the Orangery are the icing on the cake. But I also like meeting people and working for a conservation body,' he says.

Organic gardening at Belton

Having gone down the chemical route but failing dismally to control pests and diseases in the Orangery and nursery glasshouses, the decision was taken by the National Trust in 1992 to give biological agents a run for their money. The organisation was keen to take a more environmental approach, which would be beneficial to both staff and visitors, under the proviso that the new method actually worked. 'When I first came to the property, the problem had become quite bad, but it has been immensely satisfying to turn the situation round using natural means,' says Fred.

The plants speak for themselves. Open the door on a cold December morning and you cross the threshold into a different world. The moist, sweet smell of growth hits you like a slap in the face and your eyes are bombarded with every shape and texture of foliage, layer upon layer, right to the top of the glass roof. But nowhere is there the merest hint of sooty mould, the black covering on leaves and tell-tale sign of pest activity. Even the camellias, one of the first plants to to be singled out by aphids, appear glossy and dark green.

'At first we just had to be patient. The initial problem was to get a balance between biological control and pest,' Fred explains. Once an equilibrium between predator and prey is reached, it is a question of monitering to see if pest levels start increasing. If there is an outbreak, for example greenfly on *Solanum jasminoides*, Fred sprays with Savona, a non-persistent insectidal soap, based on fatty acids, then introduces the appropriate biological control the next day. 'There is an increasing amount of interest out there,' he points out. 'The public come into the Orangery and see the little cards, from which the whitefly predators emerged, hanging among the foliage. It's definitely a good thing for the Trust to put across its desire to be

Encarsia card suspended from a brugmannsia in the greenhouse.

more environmentally-friendly. However, it's not a cheap method, but the benefits far outweigh the disadvantages.'

Biological control

Enter the protected world of the Orangery at Belton and you can almost see the plants growing. Every inch of space creates a niche for one plant or other. Tall plants like the captivatingly architectural *Araucaria heterophylla* reach for the sky, while the Chinese fan palm, *Livistona chinensis*, fills in the understorey. The tiny glossy foliage of *Ficus pumila* is doing a grand job in the dense shade at the back of the Orangery, its growth remaining neat and flat against the walls. Best of all, perhaps, are the long strands of *Parthenocissus henryana* which hang down around the small circular pool in the centre of the building like the curtains around a four-poster bed.

Everything makes undeniably rapid growth in these sheltered conditions, but all manner of pests proliferate too. Whitefly, green-fly, mealybug, red spider mite, and a smattering of vine weevil – the list starts to read like a roll-call of undesirables. Fortunately they all have natural predators (listed below); Fred's dilemma is waiting for the time when he can introduce them because they are all temperature-sensitive and will not survive in the greenhouse until conditions are warm enough. He finds May a good time to start introducing them, and will continue through to September if necessary.

Close up of *Encarsia* wasp, whitefly adult and its scales, which turn black once they have been parasitised.

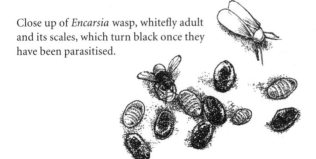

Biological controls for the greenhouse

PROBLEM	SOLUTION
Red spider mite – attacks a wide range of plants, particularly brugmansia. They suck the sap from leaves, resulting in a white, speckled appearance on foliage. Tiny webs can often be seen where infestations are severe. They reproduce at an alarming rate.	*Phytoseiulus persimilis* – a fast moving, orange mite, slightly larger than its prey but reproducing at twice its rate at temps of 18°C (65°F) and above. Supplied in a small bottle which contains adults mixed with vermiculite.
Whitefly – attacks a wide range of plants, notably fuchsia and brugmansia. Tiny white flies whose larval stage sucks sap from the undersides of leaves. These 'scales' excrete a sticky 'honeydew' on which sooty mould develops.	*Encarsia formosa* – a minute, parasitic, black and yellow wasp. Supplied on cardboard strips which contains parasitised scales, from which the predator hatches. Temps should be at least 17°C (63°F). Very sensitive to chemical residues.
Mealybug – attacks a wide range of plants, notably albizia. Small sap-sucking pests with a white, waxy covering, excreting honeydew on which sooty mould develops.	*Cryptolaemus montrouzieri* – a black and orange predatory ladybird. Supplied as adults in a bottle, they are prone to escape into the garden so Fred releases them in the Orangery in the evening when the doors are shut. Elsewhere fix netting over doors and vents. Works best at 16°C (61°F) in high humidity.
Aphid – attacks a huge range of plants, including *Solanum jasminoides*. Small sap-sucking pests that live in dense colonies, excreting honeydew and causing sooty mould. Populations increase very rapidly.	*Aphidoletes aphidimyza* – nocturnal predatory midge that lays eggs in the bodies of aphids. Supplied as black pupae, from which adults hatch. Works best at 18°C (65°F) in high humidity.
Soft scale – attacks a wide range of plants; common on citrus. Small, limpet-like insects, producing sticky honeydew and sooty mould.	*Metaphycus helvolus* – parasitic wasp, that lays eggs in the pest and also feeds on them. Supplied as adults, which live for up to two months. Requires temp of at least 20°C (68°F).
Vine weevil – attacks a range of plants. The small black flightless beetles nibble notches around margins of foliage, while comma-shaped white grubs attack roots and tubers, often leading to the death of the plant.	*Heterorhabditis* – parasite like a minute worm that enters the larva and kills it. Supplied as a powder or liquid concentrate held in a sponge to be watered onto open ground or compost in pots. Effective above soil temp 12°C (54°F).

Points to bear in mind

- Obtain biological control as soon as the pest appears.

- Introduce as soon as possible after receiving the predators.

- Be patient. Don't expect all the pests to disappear overnight because it takes time for predators to outnumber their prey.

- Some biological control agents such as *Encarsia* are extremely sensitive to pesticide residues, so refrain from using garden insecticides at least six weeks before introducing them.

- Do not be tempted to apply insecticides once you have introduced biological control as most will kill off beneficial insects as well as pests. Should you need one during the winter months, ensure it is non-persistent, such as Savona, an insectidal soap.

- Distribute the control evenly over infested plants as some spread very slowly.

- Accept some pest damage.

Importance of good husbandry in the glasshouse

High standards of hygiene are just as important in the glasshouse as they are out in the open border – maybe more so, since the naturally occuring predators are thinner on the ground in the artificial confines of the glasshouse. To avoid harbouring pests and diseases follow Fred's helpful hints:

- Inspect plants regularly; in the Orangery at Belton this is done on a weekly basis. Diseased stems are cut out and dead leaves and flowers are removed. In addition to this the soil below the plants is raked and the paths swept to remove all possible sources of infection.

- A thorough clean-up of the structure is vital to prevent pests and

Cleaning the greenhouse with water and a soft brush.

diseases overwintering and gaining a foothold in the coming season. Armed with hosepipes, soft brushes and cloths, Fred and his team set to work in late winter, washing both glass and glazing bars to remove algae, dirt and debris.

- Give adequate ventilation. This is essential in the summer months to keep temperatures down but it is also necessary in winter to increase the flow of air and keep fungal diseases such as grey mould (*Botrytis cinerea*) at bay.

- Apply shading in the summer months to reduce temperatures. (This is unnecessary in the Orangery because the leafy canopy overhead creates natural shade).

- In summer spray over the paths with water – a process known as damping down – to increase humidity and reduce temperatures. This may be necessary twice a day if it is very hot.

Leafmould

Each autumn an inordinate quantity of leaves is collected from the trees in the grounds. Most are raked up by hand, 'a good cold morning job,' Fred assures, and then piled up in the Dell, a general utility area enclosed by trees. After two years the heap has reduced by at least two thirds, and its contents metamorphosed into the most glorious, dark brown, chocolate cakey substance that crumbles into tiny pieces when you rub it through your fingers. If it looked almost edible to me, it is pure ambrosia for the plants in the Orangery, where it is used as a top dressing, applied about 5cm (2in) deep. 'The secret is to agitate the leaves at least twice during the season, otherwise they just stick together, and the layers are preserved, rather like paper,' explains Fred.

Tips

- If you have an outbreak of scale insects or mealy bugs on your houseplants, wipe them off with methylated spirit applied with cotton wool.

- Hang up yellow sticky traps in the glasshouse over winter to trap flying insects such as whiteflies. These traps are indiscriminate so remember to remove them when you introduce biological controls, otherwise your insect friends as well as your foes may meet with a sticky end!

- Use a closely woven material such as Mypex over the top of gravel on the greenhouse staging to prevent the germination of weed seeds. This in turn will help to keep your plants in pots weed-free.

Wiping away scale insects from houseplants.

Insulating the greenhouse
with bubblewrap.

- Put up bubble polythene for insulation in the winter months. When you come to remove it in spring you will find that the condensation and resultant algae will have stuck to this, making the glass behind it much easier to clean.

- Avoid erratic watering because this stresses plants. Tomatoes are especially vulnerable, resulting in split fruits or those with blackened patches.

- Keep a reservoir of water in the greenhouse for use in the winter months. Water from the hosepipe tends to be too cold, especially for delicate young seedlings.

- Invest in some cold frames. Not only are they invaluable for hardening off subjects intended for the outside borders, they will also help to overwinter marginally tender plants.

- At Belton a drag mat, fixed to the back of a mini tractor, helps to agitate the gravel, disturbing seedling weeds and preventing many from becoming established. For those with smaller areas, a good rake over twice a week would perform a similar task.

- Use a good sharp instrument, such as a knife or pair of secateurs, when taking cuttings because certain plants, especially pelargoniums, are very prone to die-back if their tissues become damaged.

Useful Addresses

For more information on organic gardening, contact the Henry Doubleday Research Association (HDRA), Ryton Organic Gardens, Coventry CV8 3LG
024 7630 3517
e-mail: enquiry@hdra.org.uk

For details of the National Trust's own peat-free potting composts, contact your nearest National Trust garden shop. Phone 01373 828 782 for more information, or visit www.nationaltrust.org.uk

Agralan Garden Products,
The Old Brickyard, Ashton Keynes,
Swindon, Wiltshire SN6 6QR
01285 860 015
– insect traps and horticultural fleeces

Atco Qualcast Ltd,
Suffolk Works, Stowmarket,
Suffolk IP14 1EY
01449 742 000
– 'quiet' shredders

Biotal Industrial Products,
5 Chiltern Close, Cardiff, Wales CF4 5DL
029 2074 7414
– wide range of environmentally friendly products, including refuges for beneficial insects

Chase Organics
(The Organic Gardening Catalogue),
Riverdene Estate, Molesey Road,
Addlestone, Hersham, Surrey KT12 4RG
01932 253 666
– wide range of garden sundries, including vegetable, herb and flower seeds, green manures and coir fibre bricks

Chiltern Seeds,
Bortree Stile, Ulverston, Cumbria LA12 7PB
01229 581 137
– wide range of seeds, many of them unusual

Defenders,
Occupation Road,
Wye, Ashford, Kent TN25 5EN
01233 813 121
– biological controls and non-chemical solutions

Green Gardener,
41 Strumpshaw Road, Brundall,
Norfolk NR13 5PG
01603 715 096
– biological controls and non-chemical solutions

Keepers Nursery,
Gallants Court, Gallants Lane,
East Farleigh, Maidstone,
Kent ME15 0LE
01622 726 465
– old and unusual top fruit cultivars

Maxicrop International,
Weldon Road, Corby,
Northants NN17 5US
01405 762 777
– seaweed extract

Poyntzfield Herb Nursery,
Black Isle, Dingwall,
Ross & Cromarty, Highland,
Scotland IV7 8LX
01381 610 352
– unusual and rare herbs and medicinal plants

Thomas Etty
(Heritage Vegetable Seed Supplier)
45 Forde Avenue,
Bromley, Kent BR1 3EU
020 8466 6785
– vegetable seeds

Wiggly Wigglers Ltd.,
Lower Blakemere Farm,
Herefordshire HR2 9PX
01981 800 391
– composters and wormeries

Index